YORK NOTES

JANE EYRE

CHARLOTTE BRONTË

NOTES BY SARAH DARRAGH

The right of Sarah Darragh to be identified as Author of this Work
has been asserted by her in accordance with the Copyright,
Designs and Patents Act 1988

YORK PRESS
322 Old Brompton Road, London SW5 9JH

PEARSON EDUCATION LIMITED
Edinburgh Gate, Harlow,
Essex CM20 2JE, United Kingdom
Associated companies, branches and representatives throughout the world

First published 1997
New edition 2002
This new and fully revised edition 2015

10 9 8 7 6 5 4 3 2 1

ISBN 978-1-4479-8217-3

Illustrations by Jérôme Brasseur, and Alan Batley (page 70 only)
Phototypeset by DTP Media

Photo credits: © iStockphoto.com /© mikedabell for page 8 bottom /
© iStockphoto.com/photovova for page 9 middle / © Silken Photography/
Shutterstock for page 11 top / © iStockphoto.com/gh19 for page 12 bottom /
Chamille White/Shutterstock for page 13 top / Destinyweddingstudio/
Shutterstock for page 16 top / ©iStockphoto.com/energyy for page 18 bottom /
© iStockphoto.com/SamBurt for page 20 top / jalcaraz/Shutterstock for page 21
top / Timmary/Shutterstock for page 25 top / ultrapro/Thinkstock for page 27
bottom / indigolotos/Thinkstock for page 31 bottom / Anna Omelchenko/
Thinkstock for page 32 bottom / Roxana Gonzalez/Thinkstock for page 33
bottom / © iStockphoto.com/vsurkov for page 36 bottom / Phil MacD
Photography/Shutterstock for page 37 bottom / muratart/Shutterstock for page
29 top / © iStockphoto.com/cezzar1981 for page 42 top / Audrey Burmakin/
Shutterstock for page 43 top / ©I Stockphoto.com/rasslava for page 45 top /
Robert74/Shutterstock for page 46 bottom / © iStockphoto.com/stanley45 for
page 49 bottom / © iStockphoto.com/Kerrick for page 57 bottom / schankz/
Shutterstock for page 58 bottom / Ishields22/Shutterstock for page 60 bottom /
lipik/Shutterstock for page 62 top / Criminalatt/Shutterstock for page 65
bottom / AnnekaS/Shutterstock for page 66 bottom / Studio64/Shutterstock for
page 68 top / Robert Morris/Alamy for page 72 bottom / © The Print Collector/
Corbis for page 74 bottom / © iStockphoto.com/count_kert for page 75 bottom
/ Denis Burden/Shutterstock for page 76 bottom / wavebreakmedia/
Shutterstock for page 85 middle

CONTENTS

PREPARING FOR ASSESSMENT

HOW WILL I BE ASSESSED ON MY WORK ON *JANE EYRE?*

All exam boards are different but whichever course you are following, your work will be examined through these four Assessment Objectives:

Assessment Objectives	Wording	Worth thinking about ...
AO1	Read, understand and respond to texts. Students should be able to: • maintain a critical style and develop an informed personal response • use textual references, including quotations, to support and illustrate interpretations.	• How well do I know what happens, what people say, do, etc.? • What do *I* think about the key ideas in the novel? • How can I support my viewpoint in a really convincing way? • What are the best quotations to use and when should I use them?
AO2	Analyse the language, form and structure used by a writer to create meanings and effects, using relevant subject terminology where appropriate.	• What specific things does the writer 'do'? What choices has Charlotte Brontë made? (Why this particular word, phrase or paragraph here? Why does this event happen at this point?) • What effects do these choices create – Anticipation? Sense of threat? Reflective mood?
AO3	Show understanding of the relationships between texts and the contexts in which they were written.	• What can I learn about society from the book? (What does it tell me about the power held by different types of people in Charlotte Brontë's day, for example?) • What was society like in Charlotte Brontë's time? Can I see it reflected in the story?
AO4	Use a range of vocabulary and sentence structures for clarity, purpose and effect, with accurate spelling and punctuation.	• How accurately and clearly do I write? • Are there small errors of grammar, spelling and punctuation I can get rid of?

Look out for the Assessment Objective labels throughout your York Notes Study Guide – these will help to focus your study and revision!

The text used in this Study Guide is the Penguin Classics edition, 2006.

HOW TO USE YOUR YORK NOTES STUDY GUIDE

You are probably wondering what is the best and most efficient way to use your York Notes Study Guide on *Jane Eyre*. Here are three possibilities:

A **step-by-step** study and revision guide	A **'dip-in' support** when you need it	A **revision guide** after you have finished the novel
Step 1: Read Part Two as you read the novel as a companion to help you study it. **Step 2:** When you need to, turn to Parts Three to Five to focus your learning. **Step 3:** Then, when you have finished use Parts Six and Seven to hone your exam skills, revise and practise for the exam.	Perhaps you know the book quite well, but you want to check your understanding and practise your exam skills? Just look for the section which you think you need most help with and go for it!	You might want to use the Notes after you have finished your study, using Parts Two to Five to check over what you have learned, and then work through Parts Six and Seven in the weeks leading up to your exam.

HOW WILL THE GUIDE HELP YOU STUDY AND REVISE?

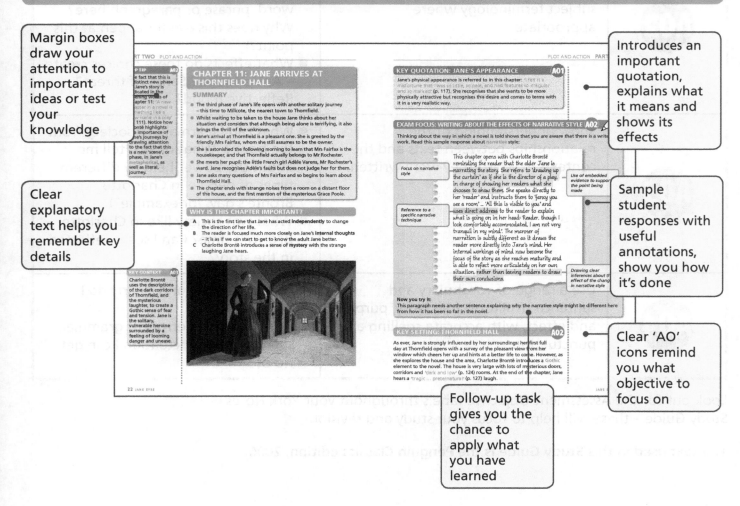

Margin boxes draw your attention to important ideas or test your knowledge

Clear explanatory text helps you remember key details

Introduces an important quotation, explains what it means and shows its effects

Sample student responses with useful annotations, show you how it's done

Clear 'AO' icons remind you what objective to focus on

Follow-up task gives you the chance to apply what you have learned

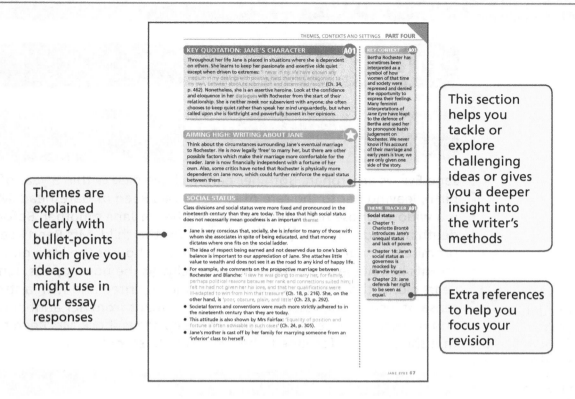

Themes are explained clearly with bullet-points which give you ideas you might use in your essay responses

This section helps you tackle or explore challenging ideas or gives you a deeper insight into the writer's methods

Extra references to help you focus your revision

Finally, each key section of the book ends with a **Progress and Revision Check**:

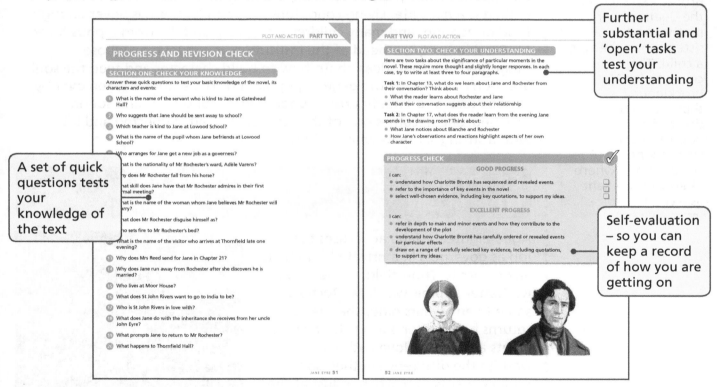

A set of quick questions tests your knowledge of the text

Further substantial and 'open' tasks test your understanding

Self-evaluation – so you can keep a record of how you are getting on

Don't forget Parts Six and Seven, with advice and practice on **improving your writing skills**:

● Focus on **difficult areas** such as **'context'** and **'inferences'**

● **Short snippets** of **other students' work** to show you how it's done (or not done!)

● Three, annotated **sample responses** to a task **at different levels**, with **expert comments**, to help you judge your own level

● **Practice questions**

● **Answers** to the **Progress and Revision Checks** and **Checkpoint** margin boxes.

Now it's up to you! Don't forget – there's even more help on our website with more sample answers, essay planners and even online tutorials. Go to www.yorknotes.com to find out more.

PLOT SUMMARY

CHAPTERS 1–4: GATESHEAD – THE ORPHANED EARLY YEARS

Jane Eyre is an orphan. Both her parents have died within a year of her birth, leaving her to the care of an aunt, Mrs Reed of Gateshead. Mrs Reed is a widow, whose husband was the brother of Jane's mother. Before his death he made his wife promise to care for the child. Mrs Reed keeps her promise only narrowly: she feeds, clothes and houses the little girl. She resents her, however, and treats her cruelly. As the novel opens, Jane is ten years old, withdrawn and unloved, but high-spirited and with a strong sense of justice. She resents the harsh treatment from her aunt and cousins, and on occasion loses her temper. These episodes shock Mrs Reed so much that she arranges for Jane to be sent away to school.

CHAPTERS 5–10: LOWOOD – SCHOOL

Jane spends eight years at Lowood, a charity boarding school. To start with, it is a hard life. Living conditions are terrible: there is never enough food or heating, and many children become ill and die from typhus fever. Mr Brocklehurst, the head of the institution, is a cruel man whose misguided religious ideas about how to build character and feed the soul are soon criticised by the general population. The school is taken over by benefactors, and Jane flourishes under better conditions and sound teaching. She becomes one of the teachers herself, respected and loved, with a strong sense of what is right.

CHAPTERS 11–27: THORNFIELD – LIFE AND LOVE BEGIN

Aged eighteen, Jane advertises for a job as governess in a private household. She comes to Thornfield, home of Mr Rochester and his ward. Mr Rochester, some twenty years older than Jane, returns home after a long absence. He meets and falls in love with Jane. Despite the difference in their social rank he wants to marry her. Just at the point when the fairy tale is about to become reality – actually at the altar – the marriage is stopped by an announcement that Mr Rochester already has a wife. Rochester shows Jane his mentally unstable wife, Bertha.

She is locked in the attic, under the supervision of Grace Poole, for her own safety and that of everyone else in the house. In spite of Mr Rochester's pleas and objections and Jane's love for him, she will not agree to be his mistress. She runs away from Thornfield.

CHAPTERS 28–35: MARSH END – ADULTHOOD AND THE ROAD TO KNOWLEDGE

Penniless and almost starving, Jane wanders the countryside looking for work and food. One night, just when she is running out of strength, she stumbles upon a house. The occupants let her in and save her from death. St John, Diana and Mary Rivers look after her and they become her family. It turns out that they are in fact her cousins. Jane receives an inheritance and insists on sharing it with them, allowing her to repay their kindness and enabling all four to become financially independent at last.

During Jane's long months away from Thornfield, Mr Rochester has never left her thoughts. She knows that whilst he has a wife living she can never be with him, and mourns the loss of their love deeply. St John proposes marriage and invites her to travel with him to India to be a missionary. She considers this, but the desire to be near Mr Rochester keeps her in England. One night, when St John is trying to push her to make a decision, she 'hears' a voice crying for her in despair.

CHAPTERS 36–8: THE JOURNEY HOME

Jane returns to Thornfield, to find that it has been destroyed by fire and the unbalanced Mrs Rochester is dead. She then goes to Ferndean Manor, where Mr Rochester, now blinded and partially crippled, is living alone. The novel ends with their marriage and the prospect of a peaceful and contented life ahead.

TOP TIP (A02)

The words 'Reader, I married him' (Ch. 38, p. 517) are the most famous in the novel. When writing about quotations, think about the way they have been written as well as what they add to the plot. This quotation is the first sentence of the final chapter. Notice how brief and simple it is, as if Jane is summarising the results of the whole of her story into one simple sentence. Could this suggest that now her journey is at an end, there is nothing more to be said?

REVISION FOCUS: PLOT DEVELOPMENT

One of the most significant elements of *Jane Eyre* is the way that Charlotte Brontë uses locations, journeys and destinations throughout the novel to link to Jane's development as a character.

Make a list of all the locations that Jane lives in, or visits, during the course of the novel, and all the journeys between these places. For each location, make notes on who she meets there and what she learns.

CHAPTER 1: THE YOUNG JANE IS ISOLATED AND ALONE

SUMMARY

- Jane Eyre is ten years old. She is an orphan, living at Gateshead Hall with her Aunt Reed and young cousins. Her uncle John Reed – her mother's brother – has recently died.

- The weather is gloomy and miserable, and as a result Jane is shut up inside the house.

- Jane is isolated and unhappy. She is not welcome in the Reed family and is treated as an outcast by her aunt and cousins. They see her as a burden rather than a welcome addition.

- She hides away behind a curtain in the library to read one of her uncle's books. She takes great pleasure in reading and often spends time in her uncle's library looking at the books.

- When she is discovered behind the curtain in the library, by her cousin John, he is cruel and abusive to her, calling her a poor unwanted orphan. He hits her so hard with the book that she almost loses consciousness.

- Jane responds by fighting back and attacking John.

- Her anger and refusal to be dominated by John are severely punished. Aunt Reed orders that she should be locked in the red-room, which used to be Jane's uncle's bedroom and is the place where he died.

KEY CONTEXT (A03)

Charlotte Brontë's mother, like Jane Eyre's, died when the author was very young. Jane is often described as reflecting many of Brontë's own life experiences.

WHY IS THIS CHAPTER IMPORTANT?

A We learn that Jane is **isolated** and **friendless** and has no immediate family.

B Jane is shown to be spirited and **independent** with a strong sense of **justice** in spite of her **lack of power**, status or friends.

C Charlotte Brontë establishes Jane's ability to **stand up against cruelty** and **unfairness** in spite of her limited **status**.

KEY THEME: ISOLATION (A01)

From the start, Jane's sense of loneliness and isolation is evident in the way she hides herself behind thick curtains in a deserted room, excluded by her aunt and cousins. She is grateful that the weather is too cold and wintery for any possibility of a walk, and spends her time studying a book, Bewick's *History of British Birds*, in which the pictures fascinate her. Note how the pictures in the book, with their descriptions of bleak, cold, isolated places, add to the creation of mood, and mirror how Jane feels.

KEY CHARACTER: JANE (A01)

It is quickly clear that Jane has a strong personality and is beginning to question the behaviour and attitudes of those around her. Although young, she refuses to be dominated by her elder, male cousin; she recognises him for the bully that he is and stands up to his cruelty. Her independence and strength of character are shown in well-defined opinions. Lashing out verbally and physically at her cousin John is a sign of Jane's strong nature and desire to be treated fairly. However, it would certainly be seen as unsuitable behaviour in a young lady, not only by those around Jane but also by Charlotte Brontë's contemporary readers.

KEY QUOTATION: JANE'S CHARACTER (A01)

This chapter introduces some of Jane's significant qualities and personality traits. When Mrs Reed and the servants discover Jane fighting with Master John, Jane hears them comment: 'Did ever anybody see such a picture of passion!' (p. 14) This establishes not only that Jane is seen to have a passionate nature by those around her, but also that this is not viewed to be an attractive or desirable quality. The idea of passion as a quality that should be fought, or hidden behind an outer show of calm, recurs throughout the novel.

TOP TIP: WRITING ABOUT LANGUAGE (A02)

Charlotte Brontë uses descriptions of settings and the weather throughout *Jane Eyre* to help establish mood and to reflect some of the major themes and ideas. In the opening description of the novel, the weather outside is cold, wet and miserable: 'near, a scene of wet lawn and storm-beat shrub, with ceaseless rain sweeping away wildly before a long and lamentable blast' (p. 10). There is pathetic fallacy in the reflection of Jane's situation in the miserable weather. If you were writing about this aspect of Chapter 1, it would be important to explain clearly how Brontë's use of pathetic fallacy influences the reader's response to Jane's circumstances as this point in the novel.

TOP TIP (A01)

A sign of a good candidate is the ability to cross-reference, for example, by providing evidence of Jane's independence from different parts of the novel. For example, Jane later takes responsibility for finding a job, and also insists that St John Rivers finds her an opportunity to work.

CHAPTER 2: JANE IN THE RED-ROOM

SUMMARY

- Jane sits alone in the red-room, thinking about the way she has been treated and how she is seen as an outsider by her family at Gateshead. She knows that she is unwanted and unloved and does not fit in.
- As darkness falls, and Jane's anger at her unjust treatment gradually turns to growing fear and panic, she starts to imagine things and becomes convinced that the room is haunted.
- She screams for help and the servants arrive. However, they are unsympathetic. Mrs Reed refuses to allow her to leave, insisting that she is thrown back into the room and the door is locked.
- Jane is eventually overcome by fear and collapses.

WHY IS THIS CHAPTER IMPORTANT?

A We learn more about how Jane is **viewed by others**, and also how she views **herself**.

B The reader becomes more involved with Jane, seeing her **unjust** and cruel treatment at first hand.

C Charlotte Brontë demonstrates Jane's ability to be passionately angry but also her **lack of power**. For a young child, she has the ability to understand and **reflect** on her situation and circumstances with good judgement and **maturity**.

KEY QUOTATION: THE THEME OF FAIRNESS (A01)

Jane recognises that it is not her fault that she is being punished, and is very angry – '"Unjust! – unjust!" said my reason' (p. 19). Jane's maturity in being able to see the truth of her situation is quite remarkable in such a young child. This desire for fairness is one of Jane's central beliefs, and a major theme of the novel.

AIMING HIGH: THE SYMBOLISM OF THE RED-ROOM ⭐

The red-room has a symbolic function, relating to the colour associations with anger and passion. Jane's pent-up fury, caused by her treatment at the hands of the Reeds, could be said to be represented by the colour red. Notice how the room is a place of darkness and is rarely visited; perhaps this represents attitudes towards passionate feelings and how they also should be hidden and locked away.

KEY CONTEXT (A03)

Charlotte Brontë was not the only writer in her family. Her brother Branwell and sisters Emily and Anne were also writers and had very active imaginations. They all spent a lot of time writing about imaginary worlds that they created in their youth. Jane can be seen to share this quality of imaginative power.

CHAPTER 3: JANE RECEIVES SOME KINDNESS

SUMMARY

- Jane wakes up in her own bed in the nursery, confused and afraid. Her 'fit' has left her weak and disorientated.
- Gradually she becomes aware that there are two people with her – Bessie and 'Mr Lloyd, an apothecary' (p. 23).
- Bessie is kind and gentle towards Jane, giving her many special treats. However, the miserable truth of her situation affects Jane so deeply that all the kindness in the world will not cheer her up.
- Mr Lloyd also treats her kindly. He visits her again the next day and questions her closely about her circumstances and obvious depression.
- However, Jane finds it difficult to explain how she feels: 'Children can feel, but they cannot analyse their feelings' (p. 29).
- In spite of this, Mr Lloyd sees enough to recognise that Jane is unhappy at Gateshead and that it would do her good to be sent away to school: 'The child ought to have a change of air and scene … nerves not in a good state' (p. 31).

WHY IS THIS CHAPTER IMPORTANT?

A Jane receives some support and **sympathy** from adults. This opens up the possibility that her attitude and reactions to her circumstances might have some support from the adult world.

B Charlotte Brontë introduces one of the themes in the novel in this chapter with Jane's childish view of **poverty**.

C The reader also learns more about Jane's **background** and how she came to live at Gateshead.

KEY FORM: NARRATIVE STYLE (A02)

The term 'narrator' refers to the character telling the story. In this case, an older, adult Jane is the narrator of *Jane Eyre*. The adult Jane recognises Mr Lloyd's ability to read the situation in a way that the child did not appreciate. He clearly agrees that her treatment at Gateshead is harsh and unfair, and is trying to help her by suggesting the idea of school.

KEY THEME: FAIRNESS (A01)

Jane is very aware of her unappealing features, and how she is unfavourably compared to Miss Georgiana ('a beauty like Miss Georgiana would be more moving in the same condition', p. 31). However, rather than accepting this, it seems that she reacts very strongly to the unfairness of such a surface judgement. The theme of being judged and rewarded or punished in life because of physical appearances begins to be addressed in this chapter.

TOP TIP (A01)

Use Jane's reactions to those living in poverty to demonstrate her developing maturity. In Chapter 3 she tells Mr Lloyd that 'I should not like to belong to poor people' (p. 30), and yet in Chapter 31 she comments of her students at the school that 'these coarsely clad little peasants are of flesh and blood as good as the scions of gentlest genealogy' (p. 413).

CHECKPOINT 1 (A01)

How does Charlotte Brontë subtly indicate to the reader that Mr Lloyd is sympathetic to Jane's situation?

CHAPTER 4: JANE MEETS MR BROCKLEHURST

SUMMARY

- Although Jane knows that Mr Lloyd has suggested to Mrs Reed that Jane be sent to school, she waits in vain for any further news.
- Christmas comes and goes – a terrible time for any child who is unloved and unwanted. She is left out of all the celebrations and has to take all her meals alone.
- Her sense of her own strength grows, however. She refuses to be bullied by John any more, and hits him hard when he once again tries to be cruel to her.
- When her aunt reprimands her, she is not intimidated and argues back.
- Eventually, Mr Brocklehurst – 'a black pillar!' (p. 38) – appears. He is the warden of Lowood charity school. Mrs Reed has been making enquiries and arrangements for Jane to be sent away.
- Jane criticises Mrs Reed, openly and honestly describing her cruelty and harsh treatment.

WHY IS THIS CHAPTER IMPORTANT?

A   The character of Mr Brocklehurst is used to introduce the theme of religion. Brocklehurst **embodies** many of the qualities that Jane recognises as **hypocritical**, particularly in those who claim to have strong religious beliefs.

B   Jane's **independence** and strong spirit are captured very clearly in her criticism of Mrs Reed. For a child at that time, in those circumstances, this could be described as extraordinary behaviour in terms of her **bravery** and **forceful nature**.

C   Jane's strength of character is becoming more **defined**. Her opinions are firmer, she expresses them more willingly, and people listen to them. Bessie's need for reassurance from Jane clearly highlights this change in their relationship.

KEY CONTEXT

Mr Brocklehurst adheres to an extreme version of the views of the Evangelical Christian movement. Charlotte Brontë had first-hand experience of this type of viewpoint during her own childhood.

KEY LANGUAGE: MR BROCKLEHURST (A01)

Mr Brocklehurst's interrogation of Jane reveals him to be harsh and cruel and guided by intense religious beliefs. To Jane's childish eyes he reminds her of the wolf in the fairy story 'Little Red Riding Hood': 'what a great nose! and what a mouth! and what large prominent teeth!' (p. 39). Jane's description of Brocklehurst shows her to be a good judge of character. The childish reference to 'Little Red Riding Hood' shows that Jane has instinctively made Brocklehurst a figure that is both threatening and and ridiculous. He is diminished in our eyes by this reaction from her.

EXAM FOCUS: WRITING ABOUT KEY MOMENTS (A01)

Selecting a particular moment from the text and thinking about that moment in terms of the novel is an important skill to develop. Read this response by a student:

> When Mr Brocklehurst leaves, Jane and Mrs Reed have their final terrible encounter. Jane's emotional but honest account of her treatment shocks her aunt and undermines her authority. The power balance has finally shifted because Jane presents the truth fairly and honestly. She tells her aunt, 'I am not deceitful: if I were, I should say I loved you; but I declare I do not love you'. Jane's character upholds the value of truth in all things. This idea is to become a central theme in the novel. As this phase of the novel draws to its conclusion there is a strong sense of Jane's developing integrity.

Shows good understanding of the moment in the text

Clear sense of where this moment fits into the novel as a whole

An appropriate quotation with strong understanding of what it highlights about Jane

Now you try it:
Compare this moment in the text with Jane's next meeting with Aunt Reed. What are the similarities and the differences between the two meetings?

KEY LANGUAGE: METAPHOR (A02)

Jane's need for and belief in love is highlighted by her behaviour towards the little doll she cherishes, despite its shortcomings. This doll serves a metaphorical function in the novel because it is a reflection of Jane: small, shoddy in appearance, almost pitiful, but still worth attention and care.

TOP TIP: WRITING ABOUT THEMES (A01)

Religion is a key theme in *Jane Eyre*. Mr Brocklehurst and Mrs Reed seem to believe that they are good Christians, but are both deeply unsympathetic characters. Does this suggest that Charlotte Brontë is criticising Christian beliefs, or is it more complex than this? How does Mr Brocklehurst compare with Helen Burns?

CHAPTER 5: JANE JOURNEYS TO LOWOOD SCHOOL

SUMMARY

- Jane travels to Lowood School, alone and friendless.
- When she arrives, Jane meets Miss Temple, one of the teachers there. She instantly recognises her as someone to admire and trust.
- Jane's first day at school is spent watching others and the proceedings of a typical day at Lowood. She is shocked by the lack of food and the strict regime that the girls have to endure.

- Jane has her first conversation with Helen Burns, and recognises another kindred spirit. She is, however, confused by Helen's acceptance of what seems to be an unjust punishment.

WHY IS THIS CHAPTER IMPORTANT?

A   The second phase of the novel opens with the first of Jane's **solitary journeys**. Solitary journeys **signpost** every change in Jane's life.

B   Jane is instantly drawn to two female **characters** – Miss Temple and Helen Burns – who will both have profound effects on her life. Miss Temple becomes a **role model** for Jane, upholding the values of **strength**, **duty** and above all **truth** to oneself, which Jane recognises and values in herself.

CHECKPOINT 2 (A01)

Why might Brontë give particular emphasis to Jane's sense of loneliness as she travels to Lowood School?

KEY CHARACTER: HELEN BURNS (A01)

Jane clearly admires Helen, but is also troubled by her. Jane immediately recognises someone with strong opinions and personal integrity, but is confused by Helen's quiet acceptance of orders and duty. Helen represents the self-sacrificing element of Christianity that Jane, even at a young age, finds difficult to accept.

AIMING HIGH: JOURNEYS ⭐

Jane Eyre is a Bildungsroman – sometimes called an 'education novel'. In a Bildungsroman, the characters start as young children who then go on a metaphorical journey towards rounded adulthood and maturity, learning many lessons along the way. *Jane Eyre* takes place in five locations, which are joined together by actual journeys. Notice how Jane travels alone from Gateshead to Lowood, to Thornfield, to Marsh End, and finally to Ferndean Manor. Each of these places has a role to play in Jane's journey towards maturity and self-acceptance, and each is marked by a solitary journey. These journeys therefore have a metaphorical as well as a literal function.

CHAPTER 6: JANE MAKES FRIENDS WITH HELEN BURNS

SUMMARY

- Jane spends her second day at Lowood School.
- She sees the cruelty of the system at Lowood, which is emphasised by the harsh weather conditions.
- The girls are given very little to eat, work long hours, have little chance to talk to one other and suffer extremely cold temperatures.
- Jane develops her relationship with Helen Burns, questioning her closely about her beliefs.
- Helen's ideas and attitudes are difficult for Jane to understand as they are so different from her own. Helen gives a detailed explanation of the value of Christian love and courage in times of pain, which Jane struggles to accept.

WHY IS THIS CHAPTER IMPORTANT?

A A key **focus** for this chapter is Helen Burns. Her attitudes towards others, in particular towards those who are cruel and unjust to her, are explained to Jane in detail. Helen's words present a detailed explanation of **New Testament Christianity**.

B Jane's desire for **independence** and **autonomy** is also developed in this chapter. In spite of feeling that she ought to be lonely and miserable at Lowood, she actually seems to be enjoying the **freedom** of life away from Gateshead.

KEY THEME: RELIGION **A01**

It becomes apparent that Helen will accept any cruelty and punishment with courage and without complaint. Jane struggles with this idea, believing that one should stand up to unjust treatment and undeserved cruelty – 'When we are struck at without a reason, we should strike back again very hard' (p. 68). Helen presents her with an alternative point of view, driven by the Christian belief that one should 'Love your enemies' (p. 69) and bear any amount of suffering in this world in order to benefit in the afterlife. Helen accepts the criticism and anger of her teachers, believing that they are right to correct and punish her for what seem to Jane to be petty and irrelevant wrongs.

> **CHECKPOINT 3** **A01**
>
> What part does the description of the weather play in our understanding of the chapter? How does it add to our understanding of Jane's circumstances and attitudes?

TOP TIP: WRITING ABOUT JANE **A01**

Identify the questions that Jane asks Helen. How does the questioning demonstrate Jane's interest in life and her own place in the world? Notice that although Jane is in awe of Helen, she does not blindly accept Helen's way of seeing the world and goes on to form her own opinions. Jane wishes to explore and understand, but she is not willing to accept things as they are. Use these questions and Jane's responses to Helen's answers to demonstrate Jane's independence of mind.

CHAPTER 7: LIFE AT LOWOOD

SUMMARY

- Jane spends the next three months trying to fit into the Lowood regime, however wrong she believes it to be.
- Far from being self-pitying, she stands up with determination to the cold and the long hours, and does her best to work hard and achieve success.
- It is very important to Jane what the teachers and other pupils think of her, and she begins to earn their respect with her quick mind and willingness to learn.
- Then the event she has most dreaded happens. Mr Brocklehurst, with his wife and daughters, comes to inspect to the school. Jane is worried that he will destroy everyone's good opinion of her by telling them 'the truth' about her from Mrs Reed.
- Mr Brocklehurst says of Jane: 'this girl is – a liar!' (p. 79). He makes her stand on a chair for a whole day, without food or drink, with a sign saying 'Liar' around her neck. He tells the rest of the school to ignore her completely.
- Jane is comforted by secret smiles from Helen and other pupils.

WHY IS THIS CHAPTER IMPORTANT?

A Charlotte Brontë demonstrates Miss Temple's gentle wisdom and **strength of spirit**. When Mr Brocklehurst criticises her for allowing the children a simple meal, she shows an underlying **disrespect for his severity**.

B In spite of the ordeal Jane goes through, she is **spiritually uplifted** by the experience. When Helen smiles at her she sees 'the effluence of fine intellect, of true courage' (p. 80) in her.

KEY THEME: RELIGIOUS HYPOCRISY (A02)

Jane assumes that Mr Brocklehurst, as the proprietor of the school, is respected and admired by all. Reading between the lines, however, his hypocrisy is clearly apparent. His wife and daughters are dressed in the finest clothes and jewels although he believes that the way to a pure soul is to punish the body: note how he complains that a girl's naturally curly hair will lead to vanity – 'that girl's hair must be cut off' (p. 76).

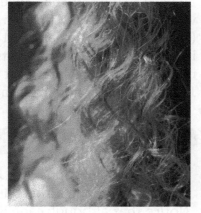

KEY CONTEXT (A03)

The strict rules of Lowood and the cruel nature of Mr Brocklehurst are drawn directly from the author's experiences at a boarding school that was founded upon strong religious principles and was, like Lowood, harsh and austere.

CHECKPOINT 4 (A01)

What is ironic about the timing of Brocklehurst's wife and daughters' visit?

CHAPTER 8: JANE'S REPUTATION IS RESTORED

SUMMARY

- Jane feels isolated and despairing, but Helen Burns comforts her by telling her that Mr Brocklehurst is not admired, respected or even liked by anyone at the school – therefore no one actually believes the accusations he has made about Jane.
- Miss Temple invites the girls to tea in her room. She questions Jane closely about her time at Gateshead, and believes her account of the cruelty she suffered there. She promises to write to Mr Lloyd to find out the truth of Jane's story.
- Jane listens to Miss Temple and Helen's intellectual discussion, observing and appreciating the warmth and understanding between them.
- Miss Temple is clearly extremely concerned about Helen's health.
- The reply from the Mr Lloyd shows that Jane's story is true, and in public Miss Temple tells the whole school that she is 'completely cleared from every imputation' (p. 88).

WHY IS THIS CHAPTER IMPORTANT?

A   The conversations between Helen and Jane show Jane struggling with **unfamiliar ideas and attitudes** which will have a strong influence on her **development** into an adult.

KEY FORM: NARRATIVE PERSPECTIVE (A02)

Narrative perspective is highlighted clearly in this chapter. As readers we are once again able to interpret what happens in a way that would not be possible for the young Jane. There is a sense of foreboding in Miss Temple's manner towards Helen: 'It was Helen her eye followed to the door; it was for her she a second time breathed a sad sigh; for her she wiped a tear from her cheek' (p. 87).

REVISION FOCUS: JANE'S DEVELOPMENT

Helen and Jane have conflicting views on the importance of the opinions of others. Whilst Jane values public approval above everything else, Helen feels that honesty and morality are more important. This conflict is eventually resolved in the adult Jane, who listens to herself first but still needs the love and respect of those she admires.

Go back over the chapters you have read so far. Make a list of the moments in the novel when the young Jane expresses a feeling, opinion or attitude about moral behaviour.

What are the key differences between the attitudes and beliefs of Jane and Helen at this point in the novel?

TOP TIP (A01)

Focus on how the writer is telling the story to the reader. Remember that the choice of first person narrator is deliberate – the older Jane is looking back at her younger self as she tells us her story.

CHAPTER 9: HELEN BURNS DIES

SUMMARY

- The better weather reflects Jane's altered state of mind. A warm spring suggests that the mood will improve.
- However, the warmth and damp bring a severe outburst of typhus fever to Lowood; the whole school becomes a hospital as more and more girls sicken and die from the infectious fever.
- Jane escapes from the illness; Helen, however, has developed consumption and is near to death. She faces this with her usual undaunted spirit, and her strength gives Jane courage.
- When Helen dies, Jane is at her side.

WHY IS THIS CHAPTER IMPORTANT?

A Jane experiences **loss** first hand for the first time.
B Once more Helen's words about her Christian beliefs are used to articulate the **theme** of religion.

KEY LANGUAGE: HELEN'S DEATH **A02**

KEY CONTEXT A03

The tender portrait of the suffering Helen Burns is thought to be based on Charlotte Brontë's eldest sister Maria, who also died from consumption (or tuberculosis).

Helen's death, an extremely moving part of the story, is described in a realistic, unemotional manner. No comment is made about Jane's feelings; a short passage describes the place where Helen is laid to rest and the simple inscription on her headstone, which one assumes was placed by Jane herself, fifteen years later. By not wallowing in the emotion, the loss of Helen is made all the more touching, as if no words are necessary or appropriate to honour her memory and the manner of her death. The reader is left with the **image** of the two girls clinging to each other for support and warmth. They are found the next morning – 'I was asleep, and Helen was – dead' (p. 98). The scene is tender and lovely on its own, needing no lengthy emotional outpourings to reinforce it.

AIMING HIGH: HELEN'S ROLE

It is important to consider the role of other characters in the novel in terms of their influence on Jane's development. Jane begins the novel with a strong sense of her own identity and self-worth. She is also extremely passionate and angered by what she sees as unfairness and cruelty. She has a strong sense of justice. Helen, on the other hand, is a perfect example of Christian charity. She advises Jane to follow the Christian doctrine of forgiveness and learn how to let go of her anger and resentment. In this way, Helen can be seen to play a crucial role in the development of the adult Jane, who remembers the lessons she learns from Helen and becomes more rational and forgiving as she grows up. For example, her conversation with Mrs Reed later in the novel can be seen to be directly influenced by what she learns from Helen about the power of mercy and forgiveness.

CHAPTER 10: JANE BECOMES AN ADULT

SUMMARY

- The devastating effects of the typhus epidemic means that the public starts to look at what is happening at Lowood. When the harsh conditions there are discovered, the school is taken over by kinder benefactors.

- Jane skims over the next eight years, six as a pupil and two as a teacher, mentioning her success and happiness at the school. Jane's independence begins to develop as she grows older.

- Jane's role model Miss Temple leaves Lowood for married life. On the afternoon of Miss Temple's wedding, Jane feels a strong sense of restlessness.

- She advertises for a job as governess. She receives a letter from Mrs Fairfax, at Thornfield Hall, offering her a position. Jane recognises that 'A phase of [her] life was closing' (p. 107).

- Bessie comes to visit Jane, telling her that her uncle came to the house some seven years before to look for her. He was on his way to the island of Madeira and could not stay long enough to find her.

- Bessie also tells Jane that the Reeds' situation is not a happy one: news which surprises neither Jane nor the reader.

WHY IS THIS CHAPTER IMPORTANT?

A The reader sees the **growth** and **development** of a more **mature** Jane.

B Jane is still **energetic**, **passionate** and **impetuous** but she has learned to **control** her feelings. The way she holds onto the letter from Thornfield rather than opening it immediately demonstrates her increased self-control.

C Her desire for **independence** and **autonomy** are shown in the way she finds herself a job as a governess.

KEY STRUCTURE: NARRATIVE HINTS (A02)

This is the second time that the narrator has mentioned distant relatives. The first time was when Jane overheard a conversation between Bessie and Abbot as a little girl. Now, it is the adult Jane who is being told of living relatives. Jane does not dwell on the fact that she has relations who may be beneficial to her, but to the careful reader this is a significant piece of information.

> **KEY CONTEXT** (A03)
>
> Charlotte Brontë and her sisters all worked as governesses. They hated the job, and the fact that it meant they had to leave their home in Haworth made them miserable. Once again, Jane is being used to explore the author's experiences.

KEY QUOTATION: JANE (A02)

Jane returns from Miss Temple's wedding feeling particularly restlessness. She says: 'I desired liberty; for liberty I gasped; for liberty I uttered a prayer; it seemed scattered on the wind then faintly blowing' (p. 102). The repetition of 'liberty' strongly reinforces the desire, along with the choice of 'gasped' as if the emotion were felt physically.

CHAPTER 11: JANE ARRIVES AT THORNFIELD HALL

SUMMARY

- The third phase of Jane's life opens with another solitary journey – this time to Millcote, the nearest town to Thornfield.
- Whilst waiting to be taken to the house Jane thinks about her situation and considers that although being alone is terrifying, it also brings the thrill of the unknown.
- Jane's arrival at Thornfield is a pleasant one. She is greeted by the friendly Mrs Fairfax, whom she still assumes to be the owner.
- She is astonished the following morning to learn that Mrs Fairfax is the housekeeper, and that Thornfield actually belongs to Mr Rochester.
- She meets her pupil: the little French girl Adèle Varens, Mr Rochester's ward. Jane recognises Adèle's faults but does not judge her for them.
- Jane asks many questions of Mrs Fairfax and so begins to learn about Thornfield Hall.
- The chapter ends with strange noises from a room on a distant floor of the house, and the first mention of the mysterious Grace Poole.

WHY IS THIS CHAPTER IMPORTANT?

A   This is the first time that Jane has acted **independently** to change the direction of her life.

B   The reader is focused much more closely on Jane's **internal thoughts** – it is as if we can start to get to know the adult Jane better.

C   Charlotte Brontë introduces a sense of **mystery** with the strange laughing Jane hears.

KEY QUOTATION: JANE'S APPEARANCE (A01)

Jane's physical appearance is referred to in this chapter: 'I felt it a misfortune that I was so little, so pale, and had features so irregular and so marked' (p. 117). She recognises that she wants to be more physically attractive but recognises this desire and comes to terms with it in a very realistic way.

EXAM FOCUS: WRITING ABOUT THE EFFECTS OF NARRATIVE STYLE (A02)

Thinking about the way in which a novel is told shows that you are aware that there is a writer at work. Read this sample response about narrative style:

Focus on narrative style	This chapter opens with Charlotte Brontë reminding the reader that the older Jane is narrating the story. She refers to 'drawing up the curtain' as if she is the director of a play, in charge of showing her readers what she chooses to show them. She speaks directly to her 'reader' and instructs them to 'fancy you see a room' ... 'All this is visible to you' and uses direct address to the reader to explain what is going on in her head: Reader, though I look comfortably accommodated, I am not very tranquil in my mind'. The manner of narration is subtly different as it draws the reader more directly into Jane's mind. Her internal workings of mind now become the focus of the story as she reaches maturity and is able to reflect more articulately on her own situation, rather than leaving readers to draw their own conclusions.	**Use of embedded evidence to support the point being made**

Reference to a specific narrative technique (positioned beside the middle of the passage)

Drawing clear inferences about the effect of the change in narrative style (positioned beside the end of the passage)

Now you try it:
This paragraph needs another sentence explaining why the narrative style might be different here from how it has been so far in the novel.

KEY SETTING: THORNFIELD HALL (A02)

As ever, Jane is strongly influenced by her surroundings: her first full day at Thornfield opens with a survey of the pleasant view from her window which cheers her up and hints at a better life to come. However, as she explores the house and the area, Charlotte Brontë introduces a Gothic element to the novel. The house is very large with lots of mysterious doors, corridors and 'dark and low' (p. 124) rooms. At the end of the chapter, Jane hears a 'tragic ... preternatural' (p. 127) laugh.

CHAPTERS 12 AND 13: JANE MEETS MR ROCHESTER

SUMMARY

- The first three months of Jane's new situation pass peacefully.
- On her way back from a walk, she meets Mr Rochester for the first time. His horse slips on the ice and falls, and Jane has to help him.
- Still unaware of who he is, she is amazed on returning home to discover that the gentleman she met is in fact her employer.
- That evening Mr Rochester sends for Adèle and Jane.
- Jane feels instantly comfortable with Mr Rochester despite his abrupt manner. She is not intimidated by him and is honest and outspoken.
- He questions her closely, refusing to flatter her although clearly impressed with her painting skills in particular. She speaks to him as an equal and matches his sharp wit and mind.
- Jane discovers from Mrs Fairfax that Mr Rochester has experienced 'Family troubles' (p. 149), and has to bear some kind of unhappiness, which partly explains why he seldom returns to Thornfield.

CHECKPOINT 5 (A01)

How is Jane's interest in Rochester revealed?

WHY IS THIS CHAPTER IMPORTANT?

A Jane's **strength of character, sharp intelligence** and refusal to be intimidated are highlighted through her meetings with Mr Rochester.

B Rochester and Jane are shown to be very similar in terms of their **mental agility and wit**.

C Mrs Fairfax gives the first hints of the **mystery** of Mr Rochester's past.

TOP TIP (A02)

The description of Jane's paintings gives an interesting insight into her character. All three present a dreamy and passionate side to Jane which intrigue Rochester when faced with the reserved and plain young governess before him. They also demonstrate her fascination with the world of the imagination.

AIMING HIGH: WRITING ABOUT LANGUAGE

Jane describes Rochester's dog Pilot as a 'Gytrash' (p. 132), or spirit dog. Remember her experience in the red-room of Chapter 3, when one of her visions in the fit was something with 'A great black dog behind him' (Ch. 3, p. 24). This idea of darkness is reinforced with Jane's description of Mr Rochester's appearance: 'He had a dark face, with stern features and a heavy brow' (p. 134). Charlotte Brontë seems to be suggesting here that there is a mysterious link or spiritual connection between the vision that the child Jane saw and what the adult Jane sees when she first meets Rochester. There is a feeling that the events in Jane's life are following some kind of predetermined course.

One of the ways Brontë represents Jane is through an extended image of airiness. Rochester remarks that Jane has 'the look of another world', and that she made him think 'unaccountably of fairy tales' and may have 'bewitched' his horse (p. 143). This idea is reflected in the sound of Jane's surname – 'Eyre'. Rochester, on the other hand, represents the opposite element: earth. He lives a far more worldly life than Jane and is more connected to society and the realities of the world than she is.

CHAPTER 14: THE DEVELOPING RELATIONSHIP BETWEEN JANE AND ROCHESTER

SUMMARY

- Now that Mr Rochester has returned to Thornfield, the house is busy with visitors.
- Jane sees him infrequently, and can never predict his manner towards her when they do meet.
- One evening he again sends for her and Adèle; the child is given a large box of gifts from Rochester's travels, and while she examines them in delight Jane and Rochester have their longest, most interesting conversation to date.
- Neither Jane nor Rochester are lost for words in their conversation. Rochester is frank and honest with Jane, as she is with him, and a large part of their dialogue explores the ways in which a relationship between master and 'paid subordinate' (p. 157) should be conducted.
- Underneath the occasionally flippant tone and wordplay, they are examining each other closely. He is intrigued by her and the effect she has on him; her honesty enables him to be honest about himself.

WHY IS THIS CHAPTER IMPORTANT?

- **A** More of Jane's **strength of character** is revealed.
- **B** Jane and Rochester discuss social equality, one of the main themes of the novel.

KEY THEME: EQUALITY (A01)

The powerful communication between Rochester and Jane highlights the equality of their minds, regardless of their positions in society. Jane is eloquent and articulate with him, and certainly not afraid to be honest: 'do you think me handsome?' – 'No, sir' (p. 154). He is refreshed and fascinated by her attitude of mind and refusal to be dominated.

KEY CONTEXT: JANE'S SOCIAL STATUS (A03)

In spite of vast differences in their social status, financial position, age and experience, Jane refuses to acknowledge that Rochester is her 'superior'. When he asks her to recognise that his 'twenty years' difference in age and a century's advance in experience' (p. 156) should be acknowledged, she states that his 'claim to superiority depends on the use you have made of your time and experience' (p. 157). For a young girl of Jane's social standing and position in this household, this would be seen as an extraordinary statement and Rochester is clearly fascinated by Jane's self-possession and strength of character.

KEY CONTEXT (A03)

In the 1800s, a person's position in society was largely dictated by family, land and money. This idea is something Jane struggles against, as she believes that worth should reflect the kind of person you are. In a sense she is showing real independence of spirit and the strength to have opinions that are different from those accepted by society.

CHAPTER 15: JANE SAVES ROCHESTER FROM A FIRE

SUMMARY

- This chapter uncovers the mystery surrounding Adèle's place at Thornfield.
- She is 'the daughter of a French opera-dancer' (p. 165), Celine Varens, one-time mistress of Mr Rochester.
- When Celine abandoned Adèle, Rochester chose to take care of her, although he does not believe she is his daughter.
- Jane does not judge Rochester for his past life, although its worldliness must be a shock for her as she has so little experience of the world. She is, however, fascinated by his attitude towards what he has done in the past and the fact that he seems to want to tell her everything.
- That night Jane is disturbed by strange noises, and a 'demoniac laugh' (p. 173) outside her door. She discovers that Rochester's bed curtains are on fire and that he is nearly unconscious from smoke inhalation.
- She wakes him, manages to put out the fire and save his life. He is both grateful and friendly to her, and this section of the novel ends with her feeling that he is becoming more fond of her.

WHY IS THIS CHAPTER IMPORTANT?

A The reader learns more about **Rochester's past**.
B Rochester's growing **attraction** for Jane is apparent in his desire to explain himself to her.

KEY CONTEXT A03

To publish as a woman in the nineteenth century was extremely difficult. Charlotte Brontë therefore published *Jane Eyre* under the pseudonym, or pen name, of Currer Bell.

KEY CHARACTER: JANE A01

Charlotte Brontë's contemporary readers may have been more critical of Mr Rochester's past behaviour than a twenty-first-century reader. However, it is an indication of Jane's truly Christian character that she loves him in spite of his mistakes rather than refusing to acknowledge them.

Her attitude to his story shows her natural morality and independence of mind. Instead of criticising him, she accepts that he has made mistakes and is more interested in his desire to change and reform.

KEY LANGUAGE: OPPOSING FORCES A02

At the end of the chapter Jane battles with the powerful feelings of joy that have been created by Rochester's behaviour towards her. The final paragraph contrasts 'billows of trouble' with 'surges of joy', 'sense' with 'delirium', and 'judgment' with 'passion' (p. 177). This contrasting language echoes the internal battles that Jane faces in her journey towards mature adulthood.

CHAPTER 16: JANE TRIES TO CURB HER FEELINGS

SUMMARY

- The morning after the fire, Jane is unsettled. Although she is sensible and realistic, she is convinced that Rochester spoke to her and looked at her as if he loved her. She is becoming increasingly fascinated by him.

- Jane questions Grace Poole about the events of the night before. Believing that Grace is the source of the strange noises and the cause of the fire, Jane is amazed that she should be so composed and hypocritical.

- Jane wonders why Rochester treats Grace as he does and even wonders, momentarily, if they might have had a relationship.

- She is surprised when she learns that Rochester has left to visit friends. Mrs Fairfax tells her about the beautiful Blanche Ingram.

- Jane comes to the decision that her suspicions about Rochester's feelings towards her are just childish fancy. She decides to overcome her emotions by painting two portraits: an imaginary one of Blanche which she makes as beautiful as possible, and a dowdy one of herself, entitled 'Portrait of a Governess, disconnected, poor, and plain' (p. 187).

CHECKPOINT 6   **A01**

What evidence is there that Jane is beginning to fall in love with Rochester?

WHY IS THIS CHAPTER IMPORTANT?

A   Jane shows her **strength of character** by refusing to entertain romantic thoughts of Rochester.

B   Jane's **position in society** is brought sharply into focus by comparison with Blanche Ingram.

KEY CHARACTER: JANE   **A02**

Jane's strength of character is clearly visible here. Although her growing love for Rochester is increasingly obvious to the reader, she refuses to fuel these feelings, and instead forces herself to stare reality in the face by painting the miniatures. This 'wholesome discipline' (p. 188) gives her some strength and provides her with a barrier with which to protect herself when Blanche Ingram eventually arrives.

TOP TIP: READING BEYOND THE NARRATOR   **A01**

Rochester's sudden departure is difficult to interpret as the reader does not know the inner workings of his mind. We therefore have to think beyond Jane's interpretation of events and judge for ourselves why he may have left Thornfield – and her – so suddenly.

KEY CONTEXT (A03)

Blanche is from a titled family, is majestic and beautiful, self confident and socially graceful. She is equal to Rochester in terms of their social position and therefore a marriage between them would be condoned. However, she is shallow and cruel. Consider what aspect of society Charlotte Brontë might be using Blanche to represent.

CHAPTER 17: BLANCHE INGRAM

SUMMARY

- After two weeks of silence, a letter announces that Rochester is about to return with a large party of guests. The whole house is to be prepared, and for three days there is a flurry of activity. Jane waits anxiously to see Rochester and Blanche Ingram.

- The mystery surrounding Grace Poole deepens as Jane overhears a whispered conversation between two maids about Grace's large salary and the difficult nature of her job.

- The evening after the arrival of the party, Mr Rochester asks Adèle and Jane to come downstairs after dinner. Jane is extremely reluctant but Rochester is adamant.

- Whilst the guests entertain themselves, Jane is able to remain unobserved and studies Blanche and Rochester closely, interpreting the relationship between them as one of courtship.

- Seeing an opportunity to escape, she slips away but is stopped in the hallway by Rochester and is unable to disguise her emotional distress.

WHY IS THIS CHAPTER IMPORTANT?

- **A** Jane recognises, and struggles with, her **feelings** for Rochester.
- **B** She observes Rochester operating as a **man of society**.
- **C** Charlotte Brontë highlights the gap between **Jane's understanding** of the situation and the **reader's knowledge** that Rochester has feelings for her.

TOP TIP (A01)

A character's response to those around them is often a good indicator of their own personality. Look at the way Blanche Ingram speaks to, and about, Adèle. What does this tell us about the kind of person she is?

KEY LANGUAGE: ROCHESTER'S LANGUAGE (A02)

Rochester's feelings for Jane are clearly visible to the reader. The considerate way in which he speaks to her, his demand that she sit with the party every evening, his sudden pause: 'Goodnight, my –' (p. 210) are all clearly the behaviour of a man in love. In contrast, the suggestive and flirtatious conversations between him and Blanche Ingram show a lack of depth and sincerity in spite of being entertaining and articulate.

KEY QUOTATION: JANE ABOUT ROCHESTER (A01)

Jane makes a very honest, articulate statement about her feelings for Rochester in this chapter. She says: 'I understand the language of his countenance and movements: though rank and wealth sever us widely, I have something in my brain and heart, in my blood and nerves, that assimilates me mentally to him.' (p. 203) This quotation demonstrates Jane's ability to see through to the truth of situations and her recognition that personality and character matter far more than material wealth and position in society.

CHAPTERS 18 AND 19: THE MYSTERIOUS FORTUNE-TELLER

SUMMARY

- During their stay, the guests play an elaborate game of charades.
- One evening, two visitors arrive at Thornfield: first a Mr Mason, then a 'beggar woman' who wishes to tell the fortunes of the young ladies.
- The guests jump at this opportunity to be entertained; Blanche, however, is clearly disturbed by what she is told.
- The fortune-teller refuses to leave without seeing Jane.
- The dialogue between the fortune-teller and Jane begins with wit and banter. The fortune-teller encourages Jane to give her opinions of the party, especially Rochester and Miss Ingram. Jane is not afraid and seems to enjoy the conversation at first.
- However, the mysterious figure then begins to describe Jane in such a way as to suggest that she knows her inner character.
- Finally Jane realises who the fortune-teller is and 'Mr Rochester [steps] out of his disguise' (Ch. 19, p. 234).
- Rochester is stunned to hear that a Mr Mason from Jamaica has arrived at Thornfield. Jane is a little surprised by Rochester's behaviour but has no time to think about it.
- At the end of the evening Rochester is chatting happily to Mason as he shows him to a guest room for the night.

WHY IS THIS CHAPTER IMPORTANT?

A Richard Mason arrives, moving the **plot** forward.
B Rochester's true **feelings** for Jane are revealed.

CHECKPOINT 7 **A01**

What is significant about the game of charades at the start of this chapter? Could it have metaphorical or symbolic significance? How does it link to the fortune-teller, and how does it link to the behaviour of Rochester, Blanche and even Jane?

TOP TIP **A01**

Writing about the way a character is presented to the reader can often include observations about their actions and reactions. For example, Jane's control and calm in the face of a visit to the 'gypsy' contrasts with the hysterical shrieks of some of the ladies, highlighting her dignity and personal integrity.

KEY CONTEXT **A03**

Jane is devastated to realise that Rochester recognises Blanche Ingram's true nature and is tormented at the idea that he will marry 'for family, perhaps political reasons; because her rank and connections suited him' (Ch. 18, p. 216). For a wealthy member of the landed gentry, marriage was seen as a means of securing further wealth. Jane rejects this idea, showing her to be progressive in her attitudes as well as perhaps rather naïve in the workings of the world.

TOP TIP: WRITING ABOUT EQUALITY · A01

Notice that the lively banter between the 'gypsy' and Jane is far superior to similar *ironic* conversations between Rochester and Blanche. Jane is clearly equal to Rochester in intellect, sense and feeling if not social status or age.

EXAM FOCUS: WRITING ABOUT THE KEY MOMENTS · A01

Being able to extract meaning from significant moments in the novel is a useful skill. Read this example response about the beginning of this chapter:

> **A clear point about the significance of this moment in the novel**
>
> Rochester reveals much of his true feelings for Jane during his conversation with her as a 'gypsy'. His words show that he is desperate to find out more about her feelings for him, and will resort to extreme ways of discovering how she feels. He asks 'what thoughts are busy in your heart', whether 'you have some secret hope', and 'is there not one face you study?'
>
> **Several useful pieces of evidence embedded into the sentence**
>
> **A clear point about the significance of the evidence that demonstrates good understanding of the text**
>
> This conversation reveals that Rochester, in spite of being far superior to Jane in terms of rank and status in that society, feels vulnerable and weak in the face of his love for her and is desperate to know how she feels about him.

Now you try it:
Select another moment from the novel that also demonstrates Rochester's vulnerability and write a paragraph in the same style.

TOP TIP · A01

Go back through Jane's conversation with the fortune-teller. Make a list of around five of the most significant things that Rochester says about Jane's character. For each one, find an example from elsewhere in the novel that supports this description.

KEY QUOTATION: THE 'GYPSY' DESCRIBES JANE'S CHARACTER · A01

Rochester describes the workings of Jane's mind with extraordinary precision: 'that still small voice which interprets the dictates of conscience' (Ch. 19, p. 233). This reveals that he knows her very well. It is also ironic as it is the 'dictates of conscience' that will cause her to leave him later in the novel.

AIMING HIGH: INTERPRETING IDEAS

Being able to look at different interpretations of an idea can show analytical skill. Rochester's actions in this chapter could demonstrate insecurity with regard to Jane's feelings and a desire to find out how she really feels about him; however, they could also be viewed as playful and possibly manipulative.

CHAPTER 20: RICHARD MASON IS ATTACKED

SUMMARY

- The household is disturbed in the night by a terrible cry, 'a savage, a sharp, a shrilly sound' (p. 238).
- Although Rochester manages to soothe everyone by claiming the noise is nothing more than a servant's nightmare, Jane is not convinced.
- She is right in her suspicions; Rochester calls her to help him once again, this time to tend to Mr Mason, who has been viciously attacked, presumably by the strange Mrs Poole.
- Jane has to stay by Mason for two hours in the dark whilst Rochester goes for a doctor. Rochester forbids Jane and Mason to speak to one another.
- Eventually Rochester returns with the doctor, and Mason is carried away. Jane and her employer walk in the gardens, and once again there is a warmth and tenderness in his manner towards her.
- However, he also asks whether she would be there to keep him company on the evening before his wedding to Miss Ingram; at this point there is sarcasm and harshness in his tone.

CHECKPOINT 8 **A01**

What do we learn about Jane from her reaction to the terrible cry in the night?

WHY IS THIS CHAPTER IMPORTANT?

A Jane is shown once more to be **resourceful** and **courageous**, especially compared to Rochester's guests.

B Rochester's increasing **dependence** on Jane is highlighted.

C Jane's **strength of character** is highlighted during the long night alone with Richard Mason.

KEY CONTEXT: GOTHIC ELEMENTS   **A03**

Charlotte Brontë uses many elements of the Gothic in this chapter. The Gothic setting with the invalid, the blood, the dark, the strange noises and mysterious threatening presence, all combine to create a sense of mystery and to highlight Jane's innocence and vulnerability.

KEY QUOTATION: ROCHESTER'S FEELINGS FOR JANE   **A01**

The strength of Rochester's feelings for Jane are shown very clearly in this chapter, but Jane still seems not to notice them. When he speaks of the 'good and bright qualities ... all fresh, healthy, without soil and without taint' (p. 252), he is clearly referring to Jane. He associates her with the natural world, possibly contrasted with the world of society that he inhabits.

CHAPTER 21: JANE RETURNS TO GATESHEAD HALL

SUMMARY

- The next day, Jane is visited by Bessie's husband Robert, who has been sent by Aunt Reed to fetch Jane back to Gateshead. Robert tells Jane that Mrs Reed's son John has led a 'very wild' (p. 255) and irresponsible life, almost bringing his mother to financial ruin. Mrs Reed has now had a stroke as a result of the news of John's death, but she cannot rest until she has spoken to her niece.

- After saying goodbye to Rochester and being made to promise to return as soon as possible, Jane hurries away. Their conversation is full of implied meaning and charged with emotion.

- At Gateshead Jane is greeted by her cousins Eliza and Georgiana, who are waiting impatiently for their mother's death so that they can resume their lives.

- Mrs Reed tells Jane that she had received a request some three years before from Jane's uncle that Jane be sent to join him in Madeira. Mrs Reed hated Jane so much that she told him 'Jane Eyre was dead' (p. 275). Although she still hates Jane, her conscience has forced her to admit to this action before she dies.

WHY IS THIS CHAPTER IMPORTANT?

A   We see Jane's great **capacity** for **forgiveness**.
B   Rochester finds it difficult to acknowledge Jane's **status as employee**.

KEY STRUCTURE: NARRATIVE HINTS (A02)

At the start of the chapter Jane refers to the 'Sympathies' that she believes exist 'between far-distant, long-absent, wholly estranged relatives' (p. 254). This could refer to the close bond she forms with the Rivers family later in the novel, prior to discovering that they are blood relatives.

KEY LANGUAGE: IMAGERY OF JANE'S DREAM (A02)

Dreams are an important image in the novel. In this chapter, Jane describes a recurring dream of a baby or young child, who is perhaps a personification of the innocence and vulnerability of Jane herself; she has to be her own support and carer because she is alone in the world.

AIMING HIGH: RELIGIOUS IDEAS

It is important to explore the way in which the fate of the Reed family is used to suggest that selfishness and cruelty can only lead to misery. This links with the theme of religion in terms of demonstrating the result of an unchristian lifestyle and attitude to others. Jane's capacity for forgiveness is clearly shown in her reactions to her relatives.

CHAPTER 22: JANE RETURNS TO THORNFIELD

SUMMARY

- Jane's journey back to Thornfield brings with it a mixture of anticipation and fear for the future. The prospect of seeking a new job does not worry her; in fact, she refuses to think that far ahead. She is too intent upon preparing herself for the pain she will feel when Rochester marries.

- Jane finally acknowledges her deep love for Rochester. She recognises that she cannot deny this and all her efforts to control her feelings will not protect her from the 'new-born agony' (p. 281) of losing him.

- Rochester is obviously delighted to see Jane, as demonstrated by his highly animated language and tone.

- Jane is welcomed by Mrs Fairfax and Adèle, and two weeks pass quietly with no sign of any wedding preparations. Jane begins to hope that the marriage is not, in fact, going to take place.

WHY IS THIS CHAPTER IMPORTANT?

A Jane undertakes another **journey**, again on her own.
B Jane and Rochester's **feelings** for each other become much clearer.

KEY LANGUAGE: USE OF TENSE

The powerful force of Jane's feelings for Rochester is intensified by the shift into the present tense as she approaches Thornfield. The effect of this technique is to remove the distance of time from Jane's narration, and make the event appear more immediate.

KEY QUOTATION: JANE

Charlotte Brontë makes explicit reference to the position of the narrator within this chapter. The reader is reminded that the older Jane is looking back and telling the story of her younger self. She asks herself, and us: 'But what is so headstrong as youth? What so blind as inexperience?' (p. 281) Using questions reinforces the idea that Jane still has a lot to learn about the world around her, and that at this point in the novel the reader has a clearer view than she does herself.

> **TOP TIP** (A01)
>
> Keep a note of the weather in important scenes. This will help you with questions about both setting and imagery. For example, notice how Jane describes the evening of her return to Thornfield as 'mild and settled' (p. 281). Perhaps this could be seen as the calm before the dramatic 'storm' of the next chapter.

> **CHECKPOINT 9** (A01)
>
> What evidence do we have of Jane's self-control in this chapter?

CHAPTER 23: ROCHESTER PROPOSES

SUMMARY

- Taking a walk in the garden on a beautiful midsummer's evening, Jane becomes aware that Rochester is there and tries to avoid him, feeling uncomfortable in his company. He has been watching her, is now apparently following her and persuades her to walk with him in the orchard.
- It is in this idyllic setting that the final truth of his feelings becomes clear; he denies any engagement to Miss Ingram and pleads instead for Jane's hand in marriage.
- At first shocked beyond belief, Jane is transported into pure joy when she realises that he is being sincere and genuinely loves her.
- She accepts his proposal. As she does so, the weather breaks and a torrential downpour forces Jane and Rochester to run for the house.
- We later learn that the tree they were standing beneath has been struck by lightning and split in two.

WHY IS THIS CHAPTER IMPORTANT?

A Rochester **proposes** to Jane.
B Jane shows how passionately she believes that **equality** should be measured by **character** rather than possessions or **social status**.

KEY QUOTATION: JANE (A01)

As Rochester continues to suggest that he will be married to Blanche and that Jane must leave, she finally breaks and challenges him: 'Do you think I can stay to become nothing to you? … Do you think, because I am poor, obscure, plain, and little, I am soulless and heartless?' (p. 292) This dramatic speech highlights Jane's strength of character as well as her ability to look at herself and her situation in life with clarity and honesty.

TOP TIP (A02)

Notice that this chapter is a moment of high drama in the plot and creates dramatic tension. Rochester's proposal should provide a happy ending for Jane, but the positioning of the proposal at this mid-point in the novel suggests that the story is not yet over.

EXAM FOCUS: WRITING ABOUT THE EFFECTS OF CHARACTER PRESENTATION

Rochester's proposal is a very significant moment in the novel. Read the following student response to Rochester's behaviour in this scene:

> It is reasonable to be slightly concerned by the way Rochester plays his game with Jane right up to the last minute: torturing her with the idea of his marriage to another. One interpretation of his behaviour is that he is forcing her into a confession of her real feelings in order to be sure that his suspicions are correct. However, another interpretation might be that he is weakened by her, and is insecure and afraid that she might not actually love him in return.
>
> Rochester's manner and language at this moment hint towards all not being well: the 'savagery' with which he holds on to Jane and his defiance of 'the world's judgment' present a cause for concern. 'He set his teeth' in determination. The sheer desperation evident in Rochester's blinkered, relentless pursual of Jane makes this scene ominous and unsettling. In spite of its containing one of the most moving and eloquent proposals in literature, the reader is left with a sense of ominous foreboding.

Offers one interpretation of Rochester's behaviour

Offers an alternative reading of Rochester, showing analytical skill

Good selection of evidence to support comments about use of language to describe Rochester's behaviour

Comment on the effect of these language choices on the reader

Now you try it:
Write another sentence linking this scene to the novel as a whole.

KEY SETTING: PATHETIC FALLACY (A02)

Setting is very important to this moment. Think about why the author chooses a beautiful evening for the proposal. Note again the pathetic fallacy in the weather conditions, echoing and reinforcing Jane's happiness. The change in the weather and the arrival of the storm hint at the metaphorical 'storm' in the characters' lives that the next few weeks will bring.

KEY LANGUAGE: USE OF SYMBOLISM (A02)

The sudden break in the weather resulting in the storm which splits the horse chestnut tree into two is a clear sign that this impending marriage has danger attached to it in some way. Jane and Rochester will be 'split' just like the tree itself.

KEY CONTEXT (A03)

A rather gloomy version of *Jane Eyre*, starring Orson Welles and Joan Fontaine, was made in 1944. It is very dark and threatening and clearly recognises what setting adds to the story.

CHAPTER 24: WEDDING PLANS

SUMMARY

- The following morning Jane is anxious to see Rochester to make sure she has not dreamed the events of the previous evening.

- Mrs Fairfax is cool towards her, having seen them embrace, and Jane asks Rochester to explain the truth to Mrs Fairfax immediately. Mrs Fairfax's reaction upsets Jane, though her worries are justified and reasonable, with a tinge of ironic warning: 'I do fear there will be something found to be different to what either you or I expect' (p. 305).

- Rochester takes Jane shopping, but she is uncomfortable with his attempts to shower her with expensive gifts. She feels that their relationship should not be transformed into a society match by such objects, and is equally uncomfortable with his repeated declarations of love.

- She manages to steer him away from sentimental behaviour, and the month leading up to the marriage passes with her in control of the situation.

WHY IS THIS CHAPTER IMPORTANT?

A Jane's **strength of character** becomes more apparent.
B **Mrs Fairfax's reaction** to the news gives a flavour of the way **society** will see her marriage to Rochester.

KEY CHARACTER: JANE (A01)

It is not easy to interpret the reasons for Jane's behaviour here. She loves Rochester desperately and completely: 'My future husband was becoming to me my whole world; and more than the world: almost my hope of heaven' (p. 316). Yet she is uncomfortable when he tries to lavish her with affection and gifts. She perhaps feels that he should love her for herself and not try to reduce the value of the relationship by making it appear the same as any other in his social circle. Also, her need to be true to herself and to be independent is a powerful aspect of her personality, not to be denied even when she is in love.

KEY THEME: EQUALITY (A01)

Jane continues to show her need for equality and a strong sense of self. She stands up to Rochester, refusing to allow him to shower her with gifts. She also decides to write to her uncle, feeling that some form of financial independence, however modest, would ease the discomfort she feels due to the gap between them.

> **CHECKPOINT 10** (A01)
>
> How does this chapter illustrate Jane's strength of character?

CHAPTER 25: A HINT OF DANGER

SUMMARY

- The day before the wedding Jane is unsettled and restless. She waits impatiently for Rochester to return home, and in the end goes to meet him.

- Eventually she tells him that she had a vivid dream which had a sense of foreboding about it. The dream again involved the idea of being burdened with a young child, and showed Jane and Rochester being separated for ever.

- She then tells him that when she woke from this dream she found in her room a strange woman with a 'savage face' (p. 327) who tore her wedding veil apart before leaving the bedroom.

- Rochester is evidently shaken by this, although he gives her a reasonable explanation for the occurrence, blaming Grace Poole once again and suggesting that Jane was half asleep and did not recognise her.

- Jane tries to appear convinced, and promises to sleep in the nursery with Adèle and Sophie, rather than remain in her own room.

> **CHECKPOINT 11** **A01**
>
> Why does Jane accept Rochester's unconvincing explanation for the vivid dream?

WHY IS THIS CHAPTER IMPORTANT?

A The **threat** of the mysterious secret in the house becomes more real.
B Jane is beginning to sense that there is **danger** ahead.

KEY FORM: NARRATIVE PERSPECTIVE **A02**

There is more going on than Jane is aware of in this chapter. The appearance of this strange woman frightens Rochester more than would be expected, given his explanation of the mystery. The reader is being made aware of this but Jane doesn't seem to notice. For us, it is clear that he has another motive for keeping Jane away from her own room – he senses a real threat to her safety and wants to be sure she is protected.

KEY SETTING: THE USE OF PATHETIC FALLACY **A02**

As so often in the novel, the weather reflects Jane's mood. Here it is overcast and stormy.

It is as if physical events are guided and influenced by spiritual, or even psychic features; the weather, Jane's dreams, and symbolic phenomena are as much involved in the course of events as real, concrete affairs. She sees the 'blood-red' disc of the moon and hears the 'melancholy wail' (p. 319) of the wind.

CHAPTER 26: THE MARRIAGE IS PREVENTED

SUMMARY

- On the day of the wedding Rochester is hurried, restless and 'grimly resolute' (p. 322).
- Jane notices two strangers who enter the church by a side door.
- When the service comes to the part which questions whether there is 'any impediment' (p. 333) to the marriage, one of the men steps forward. He is a lawyer who declares that 'Mr Rochester has a wife now living' (p. 334). He claims that this Mrs Rochester lives at Thornfield Hall and Mr Rochester is thus attempting to commit bigamy.
- It appears that Jane's uncle knows Richard Mason, the brother of Mrs Rochester, and when Jane wrote to inform him of her impending marriage the alarm was raised.
- Rochester admits that the lawyer is correct and that he is married. He also states that Jane is innocent and knew nothing of his living wife.
- Rochester leads them all to the house where we meet the first Mrs Rochester – Bertha, a mentally unstable woman, locked in an attic under the guard of Grace Poole. She violently attacks him, apparently not for the first time.
- Jane retires, alone, to her room.

WHY IS THIS CHAPTER IMPORTANT?

A The **mystery** of Thornfield is revealed.
B The **truth** of Rochester's behaviour is explained.

KEY FORM: NARRATIVE PLOTS COMING TOGETHER (A02)

Once the mystery is finally explained, much of the subtext of the story so far becomes clear. Jane's sense of a mystery at Thornfield, the sight of the strange woman in her room, the attack on Richard Mason and the unearthly laughs and noises all now make sense.

AIMING HIGH: THE FEMINIST CRITICAL READING

Rochester's behaviour at this point in the novel is often the subject of close examination. He calls upon a higher court than that of the world to judge whether he was in fact acting immorally, given his suffering since being tricked into marrying this woman for his family's financial gain. Jane does not judge him; she loves him too much. Feminist literary criticism has condemned Rochester's behaviour towards his wife and his actions. However, Charlotte Brontë leaves the reader to decide upon whether he should be censured in this way or pitied for his difficult position.

CHAPTER 27: JANE DECIDES TO LEAVE THORNFIELD

SUMMARY

- After a terrible period of time alone with her thoughts, Jane starts to look for an answer. Her conscience appears to speak to her and tell her to 'Leave Thornfield at once' (p. 343). The thought is so painful for her that she tries to turn from it, but it is the only possible solution.

- During a passionate conversation with Rochester, he pleads with her to run away with him, but she refuses.

- He tells her the full story of his marriage to Bertha Mason. His father, in order to avoid splitting his estate between Rochester and his brother, arranged Rochester's marriage with the Masons' daughter. As a rich family, the Masons offered to pay a dowry of £30,000.

- However, it soon became clear that Bertha was mentally unwell, as was her mother, and Rochester lived a terrible life with her in Jamaica before bringing her to Thornfield and shutting her away. He then ran away to Europe where he led a pleasure-seeking but unhappy life.

- When he speaks of the effect Jane had upon him, we see the full force, beauty and sincerity of his love for her. She is almost powerless to resist this, but is determined to 'keep the law given by God' (p. 365). Although it breaks her heart, she leaves secretly in the night.

WHY IS THIS CHAPTER IMPORTANT?

A We learn about Rochester's **past** life and the reasons for his behaviour.
B Jane is forced to test her **moral** and **religious principles** to the limit.
C One of the central themes of the novel – learning how to lead a moral, **Christian** life – is brought into sharp focus.

CHECKPOINT 12 **A01**

Why does Jane decide to leave Rochester?

KEY CONTEXT **A03**

Jane's adherence to a moral and religious code, at the expense of the only happiness she feels she will ever have, demonstrates the strength of her Christian beliefs. One of Jane's journeys in the novel is to find a balance between living a happy and productive life on earth whilst also living a Christian life. The opportunity presented by Rochester at this point in the novel, whilst offering her earthly happiness, cannot fit with her Christian beliefs and presents her with a terrible choice.

KEY QUOTATION: JANE'S MORALITY AND BELIEF IN GOD **A01**

Jane's bravery in the face of total despair is strongly demonstrated in this chapter. Her sense of self is an essential part of her nature, and is particularly obvious when she faces temptation: '*I care for myself. The more solitary, the more friendless, the more unsustained I am, the more I will respect myself*' (p. 365). Her main belief is clearly established: '*Do as I do: trust in God and yourself*' (p. 364). She forgives Rochester completely because she understands the circumstances and because she sees how much he loves her. He is acting under the direction of an alternative moral code, not out of immorality. In spite of this understanding, she cannot agree to his plan.

EXAM FOCUS: WRITING ABOUT CONTEXT **A03**

You may be asked to comment on the context of particular elements of the novel. Read this sample student response, commenting on the context of Rochester's first marriage:

> In this chapter Rochester explains why he got married to Bertha Mason. The reader learns that his family have arranged the marriage and have not told him that Bertha is very rich. Brontë suggests that the reason she has such a large dowry is due to her mental health issues. Rochester is only told that she is beautiful. He describes her as 'a fine woman tall, dark and majestic'. Although it would have been more common for a family like the Rochesters to influence the marriages of their children, this information increases sympathy for Rochester as he has been used by his 'avaricious, grasping' father to increase the family fortunes.

Focus on what the writer is doing

Good use of embedded evidence

Clear comment on the context of Rochester's circumstances and the effect of this on the reader

Now you try it:
Why do you think Rochester's family hid the fact of Bertha's money from him? Write another short paragraph explaining what this suggests about Rochester's situation.

TOP TIP: WRITING ABOUT OPINIONS **A01**

One of the skills of a good writer is to offer opportunities for readers to decide for themselves, to form their own opinions. Charlotte Brontë merely presents the facts – albeit from Jane's point of view – and then steps back to allow the readers to decide about the appropriateness of each character's behaviour. Don't be afraid to form your own opinions of the novel and its characters.

CHAPTERS 28 AND 29: JANE FINDS MARSH END

SUMMARY

- Jane wanders the countryside looking for work but finds nothing and no one to help her.
- After three days, she sees a candle shining in the distance. The house is her last hope; she sees the people who live there through the window, knocks and begs for help.
- The servant Hannah sends her away, but the master of the house finds her on the step and brings her inside.
- After three days of being nursed by Diana and Mary she gradually regains her strength.
- Diana and Mary are fascinated by Jane but avoid asking too many questions. Their brother is more direct, and Jane gives as much honest explanation as possible without mentioning Rochester and Thornfield.
- St John respects Jane for her honesty and integrity. Mary and Diana warm to her instantly and trust her absolutely.
- St John promises to do what he can to find her work.

WHY IS THIS CHAPTER IMPORTANT?

A It seems that **fate** has intervened and rewarded Jane's courage and morality by leading her to the house of her estranged relatives.

B For the first time, Jane is not an **outsider**, or different, or alone. She has found people who are like her, even though she doesn't yet know that they are blood relatives.

C Jane shows a more **mature** understanding of different classes of society. She is more sympathetic and defensive of **morality** regardless of social and financial position than when she was a child and told Mr Lloyd that she 'should not like to belong to poor people' (Ch. 3, p. 30).

KEY THEME: RELIGIOUS INTEGRITY (A01)

The pathos of this chapter is powerful. Jane does not wish to dwell on sordid details, but she relates enough for the reader to understand her suffering. Putting Jane, who values her independence, into extreme poverty and powerlessness highlights her integrity: she would rather suffer all this than be with the man she loves.

KEY LANGUAGE: USE OF DESCRIPTION (A02)

Note the attention to detail in the descriptions of the Rivers family and their home. Jane approves of the house: it is plain and functional, yet clean and warm. This is another example of her value judgements which care nothing for fancy things. The language used to describe the house is also functional: 'plainly-furnished … clean and neat' (Ch. 29, p. 395). The reader sees Jane's values through her reaction to the house around her.

CHECKPOINT 13 (A01)

What might the candle shining in a distant window represent?

TOP TIP (A02)

After watching them for just a few minutes, Jane feels an empathy with the women in the house: 'I seemed intimate with every lineament' (Ch. 28, p. 382). For some reason she senses a connection here: of course she is correct, and this reinforces the reader's faith in her judgement. It also reflects the comment she made in Chapter 21 about the connection, or 'sympathies' (p. 254) that exist between relatives.

CHECKPOINT 14 (A01)

What does the Rivers family's apparent lack of curiosity show about their character?

CHAPTER 30: LIFE AT MOOR HOUSE

SUMMARY

- Jane continues to enjoy the company of Diana and Mary at Marsh End, also known as Moor House. The three have remarkably similar tastes and attitudes, and a strong bond quickly develops.
- Three weeks pass, during which Jane hears nothing from St John about the promised employment.
- Jane continues to observe St John closely, and sees that he is fiercely religious. His church sermons worry her because they are so passionate and indicate that he is desperately searching for a way to devote his life wholeheartedly to God.
- Eventually he tells her that he needs someone to set up a small school for girls in the nearby village of Morton. She leaps at this opportunity, which pleases him.
- A letter comes with news of the death of the Rivers' uncle; some family disagreement means that he has not left his fortune to them but 'bequeathed every penny to the other relation' (p. 411), who remains unnamed.
- The sisters have to leave home to return to their jobs as governesses, and Jane prepares to start her school.

CHECKPOINT 15 (A01)

What effect does the news about the inheritance have on the narrative and on our understanding of the characters?

WHY IS THIS CHAPTER IMPORTANT?

A   Jane has found a **family** at last and is no longer alone.
B   The reader sees the contrast between St John's type of **religious belief** and Jane's.

KEY CHARACTER: ST JOHN RIVERS (A01)

Note St John's accurate comments regarding Jane: 'human affections and sympathies have a most powerful hold on you' (p. 409). He is a good judge of character, as this and other observations prove.

AIMING HIGH: LINKS AND CONNECTIONS

We see that the Rivers family react to life events in much the same way that Jane does. They respond sensibly to the news that they have been left without what they should reasonably have expected. Their lives would have been made much happier with even a little money, instead of which the sisters have to return to their hated professions in unfriendly households. The observant reader will, of course, have picked up the link between Jane's ailing uncle John and the Rivers family's recently deceased uncle John. However, this information, like so much else of the mystery, is left in the air until the time when all the threads of the story can be bound together.

CHAPTER 31: JANE BECOMES A TEACHER AT MORTON

SUMMARY

- Jane spends her first day as mistress of the 'bare, humble' (p. 414) school.
- When it is over she struggles with herself for feeling sad when she should be contented and happy, but concern for Rochester fills her thoughts.
- She does not regret her decision to leave Rochester, however, and knows that she is being rewarded for acting correctly. Although Jane is unhappy she feels she has chosen the right path.
- St John visits her and, guessing correctly that her past is the source of her distress, warns against giving in to temptation and encourages her to always lead a godly life.
- Miss Rosamund Oliver, the beautiful daughter of a wealthy landowner, arrives. Jane immediately notices that St John is in love with this girl, who is also apparently infatuated with him.

WHY IS THIS CHAPTER IMPORTANT?

A   Jane seems to have found a way to lead a **peaceful** existence, but is still fighting **restlessness** and **unhappiness**.

B   The **plot** takes a **pause**, allowing Jane to settle and become accustomed to a new life.

KEY CHARACTER: JANE   (A01)

Jane's admiration for Rosamund Oliver's beauty has no sense of envy about it; she can value a beautiful face sincerely, but does not put as much store by physical appearance as good character.

KEY THEME: CHRISTIAN DUTY   (A01)

There is symmetry in St John's devotion to Miss Oliver, and Jane's to Rochester. Both turn away from the love they feel: both are affected by it but choose not to give in to it. However, Jane's inevitable return to her love marks the essential difference between their understanding of Christianity. Jane believes that doing God's will should not necessarily involve self-sacrifice and torment. She believes it is possible to lead a Christian life whilst also being happy and contented.

REVISION FOCUS: FEMALE CHARACTERS

Rosamund Oliver is the last in a long list of female characters that Jane meets during the course of the novel. Make a list of all of these female characters.

For each one, write a sentence describing them and how Jane reacts to them, and also what she learns from them that helps to influence her own development.

CHECKPOINT 16 (A01)

What consolations does life as a schoolmistress offer Jane?

CHAPTER 32: ST JOHN AND JANE DISCUSS ROSAMUND OLIVER

SUMMARY

- Jane settles in well to her new life, and is soon accepted by the local people. She enjoys her job and her students.
- She finds much to be happy about, but is still tormented regularly by dreams of Rochester.
- The deep love St John feels for Rosamund Oliver becomes more apparent, as does her affection for him.
- One evening as Jane is making the finishing touches to a painting of Rosamund, St John enters. His reaction to the picture prompts Jane into a frank conversation with him.
- Jane feels that if St John and Rosamund were to marry, he could make better use of his fortune by helping the needy than by going abroad as a missionary. He acknowledges his love for Rosamund, but is determined to stick to his plan. He argues that their marriage would not work as they are such different characters.
- As St John is leaving he notices something scribbled on a scrap of Jane's drawing paper which obviously shocks him; he quickly tears it away and leaves in a hurry.

CHECKPOINT 17

Why is Rosamund Oliver introduced into the novel?

WHY IS THIS CHAPTER IMPORTANT?

A The dialogue between Jane and St John allows the reader to understand Jane's desire to find a way of leading a **happy life** as well as a **Christian life**. She doesn't believe that the two are **mutually exclusive**.

B The slip of paper is significant to the plot as the discovery of Jane's second name will lead St John to find out who she really is.

KEY THEME: LEADING A RELIGIOUS LIFE **A01**

Further exploration of St John's refusal to allow love and happiness into his life reveals some similarities with Jane, but these are not as substantial as they first appeared. He blindly follows the path of a missionary, and shows that his strong religious beliefs dominate all other feelings. Where Jane turned away from love in fear of disgrace and misery, St John chooses to deny the feelings he has for Rosamund because he has already committed himself to another road in life, whatever the personal cost.

KEY QUOTATION: ST JOHN RIVERS **A01**

St John's stern nature controls him at all times, even restricting the time he allows Jane to talk about Rosamund to him: '"go on for another quarter of an hour." And he actually took out his watch and laid it upon the table to measure the time' (p. 430). Not only does this show him to be extremely severe with himself, but Charlotte Brontë may also be hinting that his behaviour borders on the slightly ridiculous.

CHAPTER 33: JANE RECEIVES HER INHERITANCE AND HER FAMILY

SUMMARY

- The next night St John returns, having struggled through a severe snowstorm to get to Jane's cottage, clearly on important business.
- After a period of silent thought he tells her her own history, proving that he knows the truth.
- Although shocked, Jane is far more concerned with any news of Rochester he may have, and defends Rochester when St John criticises him.
- Jane is staggered to hear that there has been a country-wide search for her because she has been left a fortune of £20,000 by her uncle.
- When she hears that St John, Diana and Mary are her family – first cousins, in fact – she is delighted and immediately insists that the fortune be split four ways: it 'could never be mine in justice, though it might be in law' (p. 446).

WHY IS THIS CHAPTER IMPORTANT?

A The **plot** takes a major **leap forward** after the apparent peace of the previous two chapters.

B Jane's reaction to the news of her inheritance demonstrates how important **fairness** and **justice** are to her.

KEY CHARACTER: JANE (A01)

Jane's reaction to the news about her family and her inheritance reveal the importance of family to her. She is more excited by the idea that she is now part of a family, having been always a friendless orphan, than the fact that she is now an independently rich woman. Her refusal to accept the full amount highlights the fact that she values love, friendship and decency above wealth.

> **CHECKPOINT 18** (A01)
>
> What is interesting about Jane's readiness to divide her fortune with the Rivers?

KEY THEME: JUSTICE AND FAIRNESS (A01)

The existence of a kind of natural justice, a moral and fair system which can sometimes go against society's legal system, reminds the reader of Rochester's appeal to a higher court than that of man to judge his actions. This reinforces the idea that Jane and Rochester have similar ways of viewing the world.

KEY LANGUAGE: IMAGERY AND ST JOHN (A02)

St John's struggle through a winter snowstorm is symbolic of his cold, unfeeling manner. It also acts as a metaphor for his need to see life as a similar struggle.

CHAPTER 34: ANOTHER PROPOSAL OF MARRIAGE

SUMMARY

- Jane works hard to make Moor House ready for the return of Mary and Diana.
- The three are delighted to see each other again, and life quickly settles down into a warm and happy routine.
- St John becomes more distant, however, and appears to be studying Jane much of the time. He asks her to help him in his study of Hindustanee, a language he needs to learn before he goes to India as a missionary.
- His hold over Jane becomes more obvious, and she feels a claustrophobic need to please him, as if he is constantly judging her.
- Several months pass. Jane tries to find out what has happened to Rochester, but without success. She becomes increasingly downhearted as she waits for news.
- On one occasion, when Jane is moved to tears, St John asks her to take a walk. During this walk he asks her to come with him to India as a missionary. She agrees to this, feeling it is pointless to wait any longer for 'some impossible change in circumstances' (p. 466) which might bring her back to the man she loves.
- However, St John also wants her to marry him, but she cannot agree to this, knowing that her idea of love is so different from his.

TOP TIP (A02)

Compare the language used by Rochester and by St John when they propose to Jane. Notice how different they are in tone, in level of emotion, and in expression of their feelings.

WHY IS THIS CHAPTER IMPORTANT?

A Jane's **passionate** nature is shown once again. However, this time she seems comfortable with this part of herself and does not wish to pretend it doesn't exist.

B Jane is faced with a clear **choice** between two sides of herself.

KEY QUOTATION: JANE (A01)

Jane comments that she obeys those who she believes to have stronger personalities than her own up to the moment of 'determined revolt' (p. 462). Her interview with St John has echoes of the disagreements with Mrs Reed and Rochester, and the way in which she has been overpowered by all three only until she has passionately resisted their hold over her.

KEY LANGUAGE: IMAGERY OF FIRE (A02)

Jane remains firm in her ideas about love. Her passionate nature, which values the beauty of true love, is clearly displayed in the extended metaphor of fire she uses to reject St John's offer. She hates the idea of being 'forced to keep the fire of my nature continually low, to compel it to burn inwardly and never utter a cry, though the imprisoned flame consumed vital after vital' (p. 470): a dramatic and moving description of the horror she feels at living in a loveless marriage.

CHAPTER 35: JANE HEARS ROCHESTER'S CALL

SUMMARY

- St John retreats from Jane emotionally; although polite, he is cold and distant. She feels this deeply and continually tries to make things better, although she still refuses to be his wife.
- When Mary and Diana hear of his proposal they are equally sure that it is not a wise decision idea and that Jane should not marry him on these terms.
- However, his coldness has a marked effect on her. The day before he is to leave, she is so beaten down by his refusal to be her friend that, when he asks her one last time to change her mind, she accepts.
- At this very emotional moment she hears 'a voice somewhere cry' (p. 483) – Rochester's voice is calling to her.

TOP TIP (A01)

Think about Jane's reaction when she 'hears' Rochester's call to her. Does it suggest that her spiritual and emotional passions ultimately override the rational, pragmatic side of her nature?

WHY IS THIS CHAPTER IMPORTANT?

A   Jane is learning to **trust** her own **instincts**. In spite of Rochester not being physically present, she trusts herself enough to follow the voice she imagines she has heard.

B   The **plot** takes a **dramatic turn**.

AIMING HIGH: ANALYSING KEY MOMENTS

The moving poetry of the last section of this chapter is dramatic and designed to draw the reader into the emotion of the events and the climax of the story. Much has been written of the experience that Jane and Rochester share, that of 'hearing' each other over a long distance. Charlotte Brontë could be highlighting their spiritual connection by suggesting that Jane and Rochester share an extreme emotion at the same moment, which somehow enables them to communicate with each other. You could argue that to analyse, rather than accept, this is to reduce the force of this part of the narrative. The idea of spiritual communication reinforces the idea of a 'sympathy' between two characters, and could suggest that there is some sort of spiritual approval of their love.

KEY CONTEXT: PASSION (A03)

There is no denying that Charlotte Brontë was a romantic. Living such an emotionally impoverished existence during much of her young life appears to have filled her writing with passionate outpourings which were safer in fiction than reality. However, this particular passage of the novel cannot fail to move even the most cynical reader.

CHAPTER 36: JANE RETURNS TO THORNFIELD AGAIN

SUMMARY

- Driven by a renewed sense of purpose, Jane prepares to return to Thornfield to find out once and for all what has happened to Rochester.
- She takes another journey in the same coach which carried her to Marsh End a year before.
- After making some enquiries, she walks to Thornfield and is shocked to find it a 'blackened ruin' (p. 489).
- Hurrying back to the inn, she hears from the owner that Bertha Rochester started a fire in Jane's bed before throwing herself from the battlements.
- Rochester, who had become distraught after Jane's disappearance, saved the servants and tried to help his wife, but lost his sight and one of his hands in the process – he is 'now helpless, indeed – blind, and a cripple' (p. 494).
- The innkeeper tells Jane that Rochester now lives alone at Ferndean Manor, and she prepares to go there immediately.

WHY IS THIS CHAPTER IMPORTANT?

A We learn what has happened to **Rochester** at Thornfield during Jane's absence.

B Rochester's actions in the fire show him to be **decent** and **honourable**.

CHAPTERS 37 AND 38: ROCHESTER AND JANE MEET AGAIN

SUMMARY

- Jane's first sight of Rochester is painful and distressing. He is a changed man, scarred both physically and emotionally by the events of the past year.
- The next day is spent getting to know one another again. Rochester questions Jane about where she has been, and shows some jealousy of St John.
- Rochester repeats his proposal and Jane accepts without hesitation. They are married quietly without fuss.
- The final chapter describes the happiness of their life together.
- The very last part of Jane's narration fills in details of the ten years that have passed between the end of the novel and the narrator's telling of the story.
- Adèle is placed in a good school by Jane, and grows into a fine young woman. Diana and Mary both marry good men and lead happy lives.
- Rochester regains his sight in one eye, and is able to see his son when he is born.
- The story ends with St John Rivers: tireless devotion to his mission has weakened his health and Jane is waiting for news of his death, but she does not feel sad at this. She knows that he is contented at the prospect of meeting his Maker.

> **CHECKPOINT 19** (A01)
>
> Why might Charlotte Brontë have allowed Rochester to regain sight in one eye?

WHY IS THIS CHAPTER IMPORTANT?

- **A** The main **plot** is finalised and all the **characters** receive the endings they deserve.
- **B** The **balance** and equality between Jane and Rochester is highlighted.
- **C** The novel ends with news of St John Rivers, reinforcing the theme of **religion**.

KEY CHARACTER: MR ROCHESTER (A01)

Rochester shows remorse for his past actions and pride, and feels that God has given him a just series of punishments from which he has learned humility and repentance. When he thanks God for his fate and promises to 'lead henceforth a purer life than I have done hitherto!' (Ch. 37, p. 516), Charlotte Brontë seems to be suggesting that he has finally deserved and earned happiness.

KEY SETTING: THE DESCRIPTION OF FERNDEAN (A02)

Once again, setting is used to intensify the mood and to reflect aspects of the narrative and characters. Charlotte Brontë's description of Ferndean echoes that of Mr Rochester. Its approach is 'gloomy' and 'dark' and the path Jane takes is made difficult with 'knotty shafts and under branched arches' (Ch. 37, p. 496). The inside is also described as 'gloomy' and 'neglectful' (Ch. 37, p. 496), as if Rochester's feelings and attitude to life are being echoed in his surroundings.

EXAM FOCUS: WRITING ABOUT IMAGERY (A02)

Taking one moment from the text and considering what it might represent or suggest is a useful skill to develop. For example, look at this sample student response on the use of imagery in this chapter:

> When Jane goes in to see Rochester for the first time she asks Mary if she can take in his tray, on which stands a glass of water and candles. These items both have symbolic meanings. The water is essential for life, as Jane could be seen to be for Rochester. Humans need water for life, suggesting that he is merely existing rather than living properly without Jane in his life. Furthermore, the water is a complete contrast to the fire – as if the fire that has caused his suffering will be 'put out' by Jane bringing the metaphorical 'water'. The candles are also symbolic, representing Jane bringing 'light' to Rochester's life once again and enabling him to 'see' a future.

Introduces the symbolism of the items

Good use of a connective to introduce the development

Clear development of the analysis

Explanation of the symbolism of the candles

Now you try it:
Continue this paragraph, adding more about the eventual return of Rochester's sight.

KEY QUOTATION: JANE (A02)

One of the most famous quotations in all of nineteenth-century literature is the start of the final chapter of *Jane Eyre*: 'Reader, I married him' (Ch. 38, p. 517). This short sentence gives the reader the final piece of information that the novel has been leading to, and the happy ending the central characters have been shown to deserve. Furthermore, the simple and brief style of the sentence echoes Jane's character – it is straightforward and unfussy, communicating the most important piece of information without any unnecessary additions.

KEY CONTEXT (A03)

If you enjoyed *Jane Eyre*, you might like other books by Charlotte Brontë; *Shirley* (1849) and *Villette* (1853) are the most widely known.

KEY THEME: RELIGION (A01)

The words 'Reader, I married him' (Ch. 38, p. 517) at the start of this chapter, can tend to overshadow the paragraphs about St John, which have significant status at the end of the novel. Ending the novel with this focus reinforces Christianity as one of the predominant themes, and highlights that in the novel it is just as important as romantic love.

PROGRESS AND REVISION CHECK

SECTION ONE: CHECK YOUR KNOWLEDGE

Answer these quick questions to test your basic knowledge of the novel, its characters and events:

1. What is the name of the servant who is kind to Jane at Gateshead Hall?

2. Who suggests that Jane should be sent away to school?

3. Which teacher is kind to Jane at Lowood School?

4. What is the name of the pupil whom Jane befriends at Lowood School?

5. Who arranges for Jane get a new job as a governess?

6. What is the nationality of Mr Rochester's ward, Adèle Varens?

7. Why does Mr Rochester fall from his horse?

8. What skill does Jane have that Mr Rochester admires in their first formal meeting?

9. What is the name of the woman whom Jane believes Mr Rochester will marry?

10. What does Mr Rochester disguise himself as?

11. Who sets fire to Mr Rochester's bed?

12. What is the name of the visitor who arrives at Thornfield late one evening?

13. Why does Mrs Reed send for Jane in Chapter 21?

14. Why does Jane run away from Rochester after she discovers he is married?

15. Who lives at Moor House?

16. What does St John Rivers want to go to India to be?

17. Who is St John Rivers in love with?

18. What does Jane do with the inheritance she receives from her uncle John Eyre?

19. What prompts Jane to return to Mr Rochester?

20. What happens to Thornfield Hall?

SECTION TWO: CHECK YOUR UNDERSTANDING

Here are two tasks about the significance of particular moments in the novel. These require more thought and slightly longer responses. In each case, try to write at least three to four paragraphs.

Task 1: In Chapter 13, what do we learn about Jane and Rochester from their conversation? Think about:

● What the reader learns about Rochester and Jane
● What their conversation suggests about their relationship

Task 2: In Chapter 17, what does the reader learn from the evening Jane spends in the drawing room? Think about:

● What Jane notices about Blanche and Rochester
● How Jane's observations and reactions highlight aspects of her own character

PROGRESS CHECK

GOOD PROGRESS

I can:

● understand how Charlotte Brontë has sequenced and revealed events ☐
● refer to the importance of key events in the novel ☐
● select well-chosen evidence, including key quotations, to support my ideas. ☐

EXCELLENT PROGRESS

I can:

● refer in depth to main and minor events and how they contribute to the development of the plot ☐
● understand how Charlotte Brontë has carefully ordered or revealed events for particular effects ☐
● draw on a range of carefully selected key evidence, including quotations, to support my ideas. ☐

WHO'S WHO?

MRS REED
JANE'S AUNT BY MARRIAGE

BERTHA
THE FIRST MRS ROCHESTER

JOHN   ELIZA   GEORGIANA

GRACE POOLE
SERVANT

BESSIE
SERVANT

MR ROCHESTER

JANE EYRE

BLANCHE INGRAM
DAUGHTER OF
LOCAL LANDOWNER

MRS FAIRFAX
HOUSEKEEPER

MR BROCKLEHURST
MASTER OF LOWOOD SCHOOL

MISS TEMPLE
TEACHER

ST JOHN RIVERS
CLERGYMAN

DIANA AND MARY RIVERS

HELEN BURNS
STUDENT

JANE EYRE

JANE'S ROLE IN THE NOVEL

Jane's search for true love and happiness forms the story of the novel. During the novel, she:

- is first seen as a young orphan living with the Reed family at Gateshead Hall, where she is unhappy and treated badly by her aunt and cousins.
- is sent away to Lowood School at the age of ten. Here she meets Helen Burns and the teacher Maria Temple, both of whom she admires.
- leaves Lowood after eight years as a student and teacher to become a governess at Thornfield Hall, where she meets and falls in love with Mr Rochester.
- accepts Rochester's proposal of marriage but leaves Thornfield when it is discovered that Rochester is already married.
- finds the house of the Rivers family at Marsh End. She settles into life here and becomes a teacher at a local school. She rejects St John Rivers' proposal of marriage and life as a missionary.
- is delighted to find that the Rivers family are long-lost cousins and also that she is an heiress. She shares this fortune with them. Rivers proposes again and she almost accepts but decides to return to Thornfield.
- discovers Rochester living alone at Ferndean after Bertha has destroyed Thornfield in a fire and died. Jane and Rochester marry.

JANE'S IMPORTANCE TO THE NOVEL AS A WHOLE

Jane Eyre is the eponymous central figure of the novel and it is her journey to adulthood that forms its focus. As the novel is narrated through Jane's eyes, the reader is close to Jane and sees her perspective on the world around her. Charlotte Brontë uses Jane to highlight her views on women, society and what it means to lead a moral and happy life.

TOP TIP: WRITING ABOUT JANE (A01)

When you are writing about Jane, make sure you focus on her character and how Charlotte Brontë presents it to us. Focus on how we are shown: her well-developed sense of right and wrong from an early age (her relationship with the Reed family); her ability as a good judge of character as a child (warming instantly to Miss Temple and Helen Burns, whilst loathing Mr Brocklehurst); her ability to be independent and look after herself in spite of her naivety (finding a job, leaving Thornfield); her strength of will (standing up to Mrs Reed, leaving Rochester, refusing St John Rivers).

TOP TIP (A02)

Look carefully at the way in which the older Jane narrates her story with clarity and honesty, and is mindful of the flaws in the behaviour and character traits of her younger self.

EXAM FOCUS: WRITING ABOUT JANE

Key point	Evidence/Further meaning
● Jane is strong willed even as a child, and will assert herself when she believes she is in the right.	● 'How dare I, Mrs Reed? How dare I? Because it is the *truth*.' (Ch. 4, p. 44) ● She is prepared to argue with an adult and defend herself, even as a dependent child.
● In spite of being financially dependent, Jane is independent of spirit and has confidence in her own views.	● '*I care for myself. The more solitary, the more friendless, the more unsustained I am, the more I will respect myself.*' (Ch. 27, p. 365) ● This highlights Jane's awareness, but also her determination to look after herself.
● Jane trusts her instincts.	● She rushes back to Thornfield in spite of only 'hearing' Rochester's voice in her mind. She is shown to be right to do this, as Rochester is now free to marry.
● Her moral principles are very strong.	● 'My spirit ... is willing to do what is right' (Ch. 36, p. 485) ● This demonstrates Jane's determination to follow a moral path.

AIMING HIGH: JANE'S SOCIAL STATUS

Jane's speech to Rochester highlights that, in spite of their enormous difference in social and economic status and power, she believes that they are 'equal' – 'I have as much soul as you – and full as much heart!' (Ch. 23, p. 292) She brushes aside 'custom' and 'conventionalities' as if they were not important, and instead speaks of the importance of the 'spirit' (Ch. 23, p. 292). When assessing Jane's attitude to social status, it is important to think about Jane as a product of the society in which she lives. Consider the opportunities open to women of Jane's class and circumstances, and the expectations that would have been held for them. Having a clear understanding of the world that Jane inhabits makes it easier to understand what Charlotte Brontë is suggesting about her as a woman and as a human being.

KEY QUOTATION: JANE'S CHARACTER   A01

When St John tells Jane that she is their cousin and an heiress, she is far more interested in the former than the latter: 'This was wealth indeed! – wealth to the heart!' (Ch. 33, p. 444). She calls the news of the fortune 'ponderous' and 'sobering' and is much more excited for the 'blessing, bright, vivid, and exhilarating' news that she finally has a family of her own (Ch. 33, p. 444).

MR ROCHESTER

MR ROCHESTER'S ROLE IN THE NOVEL

Edward Rochester is the owner of Thornfield Hall and the man Jane falls in love with. During the novel he:

- meets Jane during one of his rare returns to Thornfield. He spends most of his time abroad, trying to forget the betrayal of his family and his miserable marriage to Bertha. He gets to know Jane and falls in love with her.

- invites a party of guests to Thornfield, including Blanche Ingram, who many (including Jane) believe he will marry. He disguises himself as a fortune-teller in an attempt to find out more about Jane and how she feels about him.

- proposes to Jane although his first wife Bertha is still alive. When the first marriage is discovered, he tries to persuade Jane to go away with him and live as his mistress.

- rescues the servants from a fire at Thornfield caused by Bertha. Bertha dies in the fire and Rochester is blinded and loses one of his hands.

- is finally reunited with Jane when she returns and finds him at Ferndean Manor. They marry and later Rochester regains the sight in one eye which enables him to see their son when he is born.

KEY CONTEXT (A03)

Charlotte Brontë is drawing upon Romantic notions of a Byronic hero in her presentation of Rochester. He is presented as dark, brooding and vaguely menacing; he has hidden depths and secrets, and he is strong, determined and passionate.

ROCHESTER'S IMPORTANCE TO THE NOVEL AS A WHOLE

Rochester represents the passionate, fiery side of Jane that she searches for. He is shown to be equal to Jane in wit and intelligence, and worthy of her love. He also represents the outside world of which Jane has little experience; he is widely travelled and operates in a completely different social sphere to Jane. He redeems himself by his actions in the fire at Thornfield, as well as by recognising and appreciating Jane's true qualities.

AIMING HIGH: ROCHESTER'S DEVELOPMENT

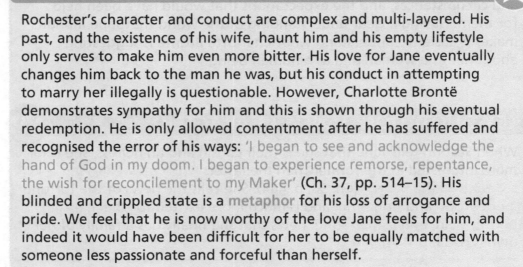

Rochester's character and conduct are complex and multi-layered. His past, and the existence of his wife, haunt him and his empty lifestyle only serves to make him even more bitter. His love for Jane eventually changes him back to the man he was, but his conduct in attempting to marry her illegally is questionable. However, Charlotte Brontë demonstrates sympathy for him and this is shown through his eventual redemption. He is only allowed contentment after he has suffered and recognised the error of his ways: 'I began to see and acknowledge the hand of God in my doom. I began to experience remorse, repentance, the wish for reconcilement to my Maker' (Ch. 37, pp. 514–15). His blinded and crippled state is a metaphor for his loss of arrogance and pride. We feel that he is now worthy of the love Jane feels for him, and indeed it would have been difficult for her to be equally matched with someone less passionate and forceful than herself.

EXAM FOCUS: WRITING ABOUT ROCHESTER

Key point	Evidence/Further meaning
• Rochester is clearly fascinated by Jane from the moment he meets her.	• He questions her closely at their second meeting: 'he searched my face with eyes that I saw were dark, irate, and piercing' (Ch. 13, p. 142). • There is a darkness and mystery about him, as well as some hidden anger.
• His past and his present circumstances are a heavy burden to bear.	• Mrs Fairfax says that he has 'peculiarities of temper' that 'allowance should be made' for 'because he has painful thoughts' (Ch. 13, p. 149). • Those around him indulge his irrational behaviour.
• He is haunted by his past and by the responsibility he has towards Bertha. However, he is still determined to find a way to marry Jane.	• 'Will I not guard, and cherish, and solace her? Is there not love in my heart, and constancy in my resolves? It will expiate at God's tribunal. I know my Maker sanctions what I do.' (Ch. 23, p. 295) • His desperation to marry Jane makes him attempt to defy the law.
• He attempts to save Bertha from the fire in spite of the misery she has caused him.	• 'It was all his own courage, and a body may say, his kindness, in a way, ma'am: he wouldn't leave the house till everyone else was out before him.' (Ch. 36, p. 494) • His actions in the fire redeem him from his previous moral conduct.

TOP TIP: WRITING ABOUT IMAGERY (A01)

Make sure you pay attention to the imagery and symbolism Charlotte Brontë uses to bring out her characters' personalities. Notice how fire is closely connected with fiery and passionate Rochester, and compare this with the cold and snow imagery that is connected with reserved and controlled St John Rivers. There is an argument that the two men represent conflicting aspects of Jane's character, and that her eventual contentment comes from the way in which she reconciles these two aspects of her own personality.

BERTHA ROCHESTER

BERTHA'S ROLE IN THE NOVEL

Bertha Rochester is Mr Rochester's first wife. His family persuaded him to marry her in order to obtain her large fortune. He later discovers that she is mentally unstable. During the novel she:

- is hidden away at Thornfield, cared for by Grace Poole.
- attacks Rochester by setting fire to his bed.
- attacks her brother Richard when he comes to visit.
- visits Jane's room and rips up her wedding veil.
- sets fire to Jane's bed after she has left Thornfield before throwing herself from the battlements of the house as it burns.

EXAM FOCUS: WRITING ABOUT BERTHA

Key point	Evidence/Further meaning
• Her presence is felt powerfully from the moment Jane enters Thornfield.	• 'It was a curious laugh – distinct, formal, mirthless.' (Ch. 11, p. 26) • This hints at the dangerous effect that Bertha will have on Jane's life.
• Her actions seem to suggest that she knows what is going on at Thornfield.	• She sets fire to Rochester's and Jane's beds, which could be seen as symbolic of attempting to destroy their love for each other.
• She is wordlessly violent, communicating her feelings through actions.	• She attacks both her brother and Rochester as well as tearing Jane's veil and starting two fires.

TOP TIP (A01)

Make sure you focus on Bertha as a plot device, whose actions drive the plot forward as well as providing the sense of Gothic mystery and threat. She provides the conflict which must be resolved in order for Rochester and Jane to be together.

AIMING HIGH: BERTHA AS JANE'S ANTITHESIS

Bertha is an elusive figure who never speaks and is only seen twice, yet dominates the central action of the novel. In order to aim high, think about what Bertha might symbolise in the novel. She is associated with passionate behaviour and violent actions, very much the antithesis to Jane's attempt to control her feelings. She communicates through fire and only surfaces during the night, which is a direct contrast to Jane's 'airy' associations and love of the wild outdoors. Perhaps Bertha symbolises the passionate, fiery side of Jane's nature which she tries hard to suppress.

ST JOHN RIVERS

Along with his sisters Diana and Mary, St John helps to nurse Jane back to health when she arrives at Marsh End. During the novel he:

- arranges for Jane to become the teacher at a local charitable school.
- is in love with the daughter of a local landowner, Rosamund Oliver, but refuses to act on his feelings as he believes she will not make a good missionary's wife.
- proposes to Jane twice but she rejects him, knowing that he doesn't love her.
- writes a last letter to Jane suggesting that he is dying but saying he is contented as he will soon be closer to God.

TOP TIP: WRITING ABOUT ST JOHN RIVERS (A01)

Think about how Charlotte Brontë highlights St John's austerity. His beliefs are so inflexible that he allows for no human faults. Jane clearly struggles with this aspect of him, because she can see his kindness in his devotion to helping others, no matter what the personal sacrifice. Jane believes that she can serve God by enjoying the life that He gave her, whereas St John believes that the only way to ensure a place in heaven is to devote your life to others at the expense of your own comfort and happiness.

TOP TIP (A01)

Notice how St John represents a very strong form of religious belief. He can be contrasted with Rochester in terms of how he represents a cold determination to follow Christian doctrine at the expense of personal happiness and love.

MRS REED

Mrs Reed is the widow of Jane's uncle. She lives at Gateshead Hall with her three children: John, Eliza and Georgiana. Her late husband asked her to look after Jane and to treat her as a daughter. During the novel she:

- is harsh and cruel to Jane, locking her in the red-room for attacking John, without listening to her explanation.
- arranges for Mr Brocklehurst to take Jane to Lowood School.
- has a stroke as a result of the disgrace and financial ruin that her son John brings on the family.
- asks to see Jane when she is dying and tells her that her uncle is still alive and had tried to contact Jane. She told him that Jane was dead.

TOP TIP: WRITING ABOUT MRS REED (A01)

Focus on what Mrs Reed's actions and words show of her character. She is clearly a stern and cold woman who has no feelings for Jane at all. After sending Jane away to school she makes no contact with her until Jane is an adult and Mrs Reed is on her deathbed. In spite of being close to death she refuses to be reconciled with Jane, indeed managing to blame her: 'You were born, I think, to be my torment: my last hour is racked by the recollection of a deed which, but for you, I should never have been tempted to commit' (Ch. 21, p. 275).

HELEN BURNS

Helen is a student at Lowood School and Jane's first friend. She has strong Christian beliefs. During the novel she:

- shows kindness to Jane when Mr Brocklehurst calls her a liar.
- explains her Christian beliefs to Jane.
- becomes ill and dies at school. Fifteen years later Jane erects a gravestone in her memory.

TOP TIP (A01)

Helen introduces the ideas of religious sacrifice which run through the novel. She believes that it is her duty to suffer patiently whatever punishment she is given. Jane reacts strongly to this: 'I could not comprehend this doctrine of endurance' (Ch. 6, p. 67).

AIMING HIGH: HELEN BURNS

Make sure you can show how Jane is instantly drawn to Helen when she arrives at Lowood. Note that Helen's illness is announced before we even meet her: 'the sound of a cough close behind me made me turn my head' (Ch. 5, p. 59). She is to have a profound effect on Jane's life in many ways. She is the first person ever to be consistently kind to Jane – her first friend, in fact. She is intelligent and well read: qualities Jane admires very much as they lead to independence of mind. Her death affects Jane profoundly, and is possibly one of the reasons she is never mentioned again.

MISS TEMPLE

Miss Temple is a teacher at Lowood School. She shows great kindness to both Jane and Helen. During the novel, she:

- defends the students when Mr Brocklehurst's regime shows his cruelty and harshness.
- laughs at Mr Brocklehurst's instructions to cut the girls' hair.
- befriends Jane and Helen.
- eventually marries and leaves Lowood.

TOP TIP: WRITING ABOUT MISS TEMPLE (A01)

Miss Temple is one of the several female characters that Jane meets on her journey and who help to influence her development. She shows bravery when she stands up to Mr Brocklehurst and defends the girls against his strict regime, not afraid to defend the children when she feels he is inflicting unnecessary suffering. She is thoughtful, sensitive and intelligent, recognising Helen's illness and showing kindness and concern for both her and Jane.

Miss Temple demonstrates the qualities that Jane admires: 'to her instruction I owed the best part of my acquirements ... she had stood me in the stead of mother, governess, and latterly, companion' (Ch. 10, p. 100). When Miss Temple leaves Lowood to be married, Jane feels the loss of 'the serene atmosphere I had been breathing in her vicinity' (Ch. 10, p. 101).

MR BROCKLEHURST

Mr Brocklehurst is the superintendent of Lowood School. During the novel, he:

- is invited to Gateshead Hall by Mrs Reed to meet Jane and arrange for her to become a pupil at his school.
- visits the school with his spoiled daughters and talks about his firm religious convictions.
- announces that Jane is a liar and should be punished by being made to stand on a stool all day and being ignored by the staff and pupils.

AIMING HIGH: MR BROCKLEHURST

You could argue that Mr Brocklehurst is more important for what he represents than who he is. His religious doctrines are harsh but are also shown to be false and hypocritical. His own daughters are not made to follow the same strictures and Miss Temple clearly finds him ridiculous. For Jane, he represents the kind of insincerity and lack of honesty that she finds abhorrent.

> **TOP TIP** (A02)
>
> Make sure you can write about the role of minor characters. All the characters in the novel perform a function and are there to add something to the themes and ideas and therefore help the reader understand Jane.

MRS FAIRFAX

Mrs Fairfax is the housekeeper at Thornfield Hall. During the novel, she:

- befriends Jane and is kind to her when she arrives at Thornfield.
- gives Jane some hints about Mr Rochester's troubled past.
- is shocked and concerned about Jane's relationship with Rochester.
- is sent away from Thornfield with a generous pension when Jane leaves.

GRACE POOLE

Grace Poole is the servant employed by Rochester to look after Bertha. During the novel, she:

- is used by Mrs Fairfax and Rochester as the reason for the noises Jane hears.
- is known to drink alcohol, which enables Bertha to escape from her and roam Thornfield at night.

TOP TIP: GRACE POOLE AND THE GOTHIC (A03)

When writing about the Gothic elements in *Jane Eyre*, Grace Poole is a useful character to include as she adds to the sense of mystery and threat underlying Jane's first months at Thornfield. The revelation of her status as nurse / jailor only comes when the full reality of Bertha's presence is shown on the day of the wedding.

DIANA AND MARY RIVERS

Diana and Mary are St John's sisters, who help to bring Jane back to health when she arrives at Marsh End. They:

- are both governesses in wealthy households.
- become like sisters to Jane.

TOP TIP: WRITING ABOUT DIANA AND MARY (A01)

In terms of both plot and character development, Diana and Mary have a significant function in aiding Jane to reach maturity and complete her sense of self. They are very similar to Jane: educated, interesting, kind and gentle. Jane blossoms in their company, becoming more relaxed and confident because she is liked and respected by those whom she likes and respects. Think about where they appear in the novel in terms of Jane's development as a fully rounded character.

BLANCHE INGRAM

Miss Ingram is the beautiful, self-possessed woman who Jane believes is to marry Rochester. During the novel, she:

- visits Thornfield and shows herself to be accomplished and beautiful.
- shows her malice and arrogance through her comments about Jane and Adèle.
- is tricked by Rochester into believing that he has little fortune, proving that she only wanted to marry him for his money.

KEY CONTEXT (A03)

Diana and Mary's importance to Jane could be seen as resonant of Charlotte Brontë's relationship with her sisters Emily and Anne. They become Jane's sisters in mind if not in blood tie, although it transpires that they are, in fact, related. She describes their relationship as the 'perfect congeniality of tastes, sentiments and principles' (Ch. 30, p. 402).

TOP TIP: WRITING ABOUT BLANCHE INGRAM (A01)

Think about the contrast between Jane and Blanche. Although Blanche shows a superficial cleverness, she is also arrogant, vain and malicious. She is no match, in Mr Rochester's eyes, for Jane's intellect, modesty and pragmatism; indeed, she is not to Mr Rochester's taste at all. She is as loud and brash as Jane is deferential. In many ways they are polar opposites of each other.

PROGRESS AND REVISION CHECK

SECTION ONE: CHECK YOUR KNOWLEDGE

Answer these quick questions to test your basic knowledge of the novel's characters:

1. What is the name of Mrs Reed's son?
2. What is the name of the housekeeper of Thornfield Hall?
3. Who is Richard Mason?
4. Who is the mysterious servant who looks after Bertha Rochester?
5. What are the names of St John Rivers' two sisters?
6. Who makes friends with Jane when she goes to Lowood School?
7. What is the name of Jane's pupil at Thornfield Hall?
8. Which teacher does Jane really admire?
9. What is the name of the young woman who Jane thinks Mr Rochester is going to marry?
10. What is the name of the servant who looks after Jane at Gateshead Hall?

SECTION TWO: CHECK YOUR UNDERSTANDING

Here is a task which requires a slightly longer response. Try to write at least three or four paragraphs.

Task: Jane meets several female characters during the course of the novel. Select one female character and write about:

- what the relationship between Jane and this character is like
- what Jane learns from this character and why they are useful in the novel as a whole.

PROGRESS CHECK

GOOD PROGRESS

I can:

- explain the significance of the main characters in how the action develops ☐
- refer to how they are described by Charlotte Brontë and how this affects the way we see them. ☐

EXCELLENT PROGRESS

I can:

- analyse in detail how Charlotte Brontë has shaped and developed characters over the course of the novel ☐
- infer key ideas, themes and issues from the ways characters and relationships are presented by Charlotte Brontë. ☐

THEMES

OVERVIEW

Although several of the major themes are discussed below, this is by no means a definitive list and it would be useful to consider how many others there are. It is often difficult to think about a theme in isolation and you will probably find that strands of one theme tend to overlap with another.

LOVE AND MARRIAGE

THEME TRACKER A01

Love and marriage

- Chapter 18: Jane describes the relationship between Rochester and Blanche Ingram.

- Chapter 27: Rochester explains what drew him to Jane.

- Chapter 38: Jane describes the beauty of her marriage with Rochester.

Jane Eyre is essentially a love story and the relationship between Jane and Rochester is the main focus of the plot. On the surface, Charlotte Brontë is making use of a very simple plot line which is familiar throughout the history of storytelling – boy meets girl, boy loses girl, boy and girl are reunited after some hardship and eventually live happily ever after.

- Jane and Rochester are clearly well suited, but have to be separated in order to experience a time of individual character development before they can finally enjoy peace together.

- Jane needs to become Rochester's equal in independence and maturity: her physical struggle and emotional torment strengthen her character and turn her from a naive girl into a woman.

- Rochester commits a selfless act and proves that he has seen the error of his former ways in order to become a whole person again. He now needs Jane as much as she needs him.

- Ironically, he is a better man without his sight and his hand than when he was whole, and Jane loves him more when he is vulnerable than when he was fiercely independent.

REVISION FOCUS: TRACKING THE THEME OF LOVE AND MARRIAGE

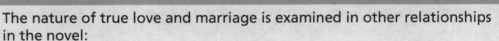

The nature of true love and marriage is examined in other relationships in the novel:

- Aunt Reed's refusal to keep the promise made to her dead husband
- The scornful description of cousin Georgiana's 'advantageous match' (Ch. 22, p. 279)
- The prospect of a union between Rochester and Blanche Ingram, clearly advantageous financially and socially, but not founded in love
- St John Rivers' love for Rosamund Oliver which is described as possibly a surface attraction: 'While something in me ... is acutely sensible to her charms, something else is as deeply impressed with her defects' (Ch. 32, p. 431)
- The prospect of a marriage of duty and convenience between Jane and St John, passionately rejected by Jane: 'I scorn your idea of love ... I scorn the counterfeit sentiment you offer' (Ch. 34, p. 471)

Create a table showing these examples and then add the connections to the main love story between Jane and Rochester.

KEY QUOTATION: INTERNAL BEAUTY   (A01)

An important idea in the novel is that internal is more important than external beauty. Jane and Rochester are both passionate characters who have an enormous capacity to love. Neither one of them is particularly physically attractive, which is important to the theme because Charlotte Brontë suggests that beauty often deflects attention away from character, and she is highlighting that surface appearances are not important. For Jane, love is closely linked with equality, respect and affinity: 'I feel akin to him – I understand the language of his countenance and movements: though rank and wealth sever us widely, I have something in my brain and heart, in my blood and nerves, that assimilates me mentally to him ... I must, then, repeat continually that we are for ever sundered – and yet, while I breathe and think, I must love him.' (Ch. 17, pp. 203–4)

KEY CONTEXT   (A03)

Wuthering Heights, by Charlotte Brontë's sister Emily, is another powerful and dramatic love story. Heathcliff, the male protagonist in *Wuthering Heights*, shares some similarities with Rochester in that both are strong, brooding male characters.

RELIGION

The nature of Christianity and religious ideas and images are referred to frequently and are an integral theme of the novel. Jane has strong religious beliefs and her system of value judgement is founded on a strict moral code. Think about examples in the text where she displays the following attributes:

- Putting others before herself and not being judgemental
- Valuing good character more highly than surface appearance
- Working hard to deserve the good opinion of others

There are several other characters in the novel who demonstrate their religious beliefs. It is interesting to note Jane's reaction to each of them, and that whilst she can admire some and condemn others, she adheres to her own system of belief throughout. Think about her reaction to the following:

- Helen Burns, who displays the doctrine of 'turning the other cheek'. She suffers terribly and never complains, even when unfairly treated
- Mr Brocklehurst, who is fearsome and tyrannical, and uses religion as a justification for cruelty and neglect
- Eliza Reed, a cold and fervent woman who gives her life to God by becoming a nun. Jane views this with detached cynicism: 'You are not without sense, cousin Eliza; but what you have, I suppose, in another year will be walled up alive in a French convent' (Ch. 22, p. 279)
- St John Rivers, a passionately religious man who is on a quest for the best way to give his life to God

THEME TRACKER (A01)

Religion

- Chapter 6: Helen Burns explains her Christian beliefs and attitudes.
- Chapter 27: Jane battles with her conscience.
- Chapter 32: St John describes his attitudes towards religious service.

KEY CONTEXT (A03)

The religious **context** of the novel is significant because religion was far more a part of everyone's day-to-day life at the time the novel was written than it is now. Nearly everyone went to church, said prayers at bedtime and studied the Bible. Religion played an important role in Charlotte Brontë's life – her father was a parson and the family lived in the parsonage in Haworth.

THEME TRACKER (A01)

Female independence

- Chapter 4: Jane stands up to Mrs Reed.
- Chapter 10: Jane finds herself a new occupation.
- Chapter 34: Jane stands up to St John Rivers.

TOP TIP (A01)

Think about what Mrs Reed's presence enables us to learn about Jane. The young Jane is able to show how she responds to senseless cruelty, and the adult Jane is able to demonstrate her ability to forgive: 'I long earnestly to be reconciled to you now: kiss me, aunt' (Ch. 21, p. 276).

KEY QUOTATION: FULFILMENT (A01)

In the end Jane chooses to believe that she is entitled to lead a happy life and that in doing so she can still serve God: 'if ever I thought a good thought – if ever I prayed a sincere and blameless prayer – if ever I wished a righteous wish – I am rewarded now. To be your wife is, for me, to be as happy as I can be on earth' (Ch. 37, p. 513). She has finally found the destination she has been searching for: to be a good Christian by leading a happy and fulfilled life.

FEMALE INDEPENDENCE

The novel explores the idea of a woman alone, in charge of her own life and making her own decisions.

- Because Jane is alone in the world, she has to forge her own path in life and be responsible for herself.
- However, Jane has a clear view of the reality of her circumstances: 'I want this because it is of no use wanting anything better' (Ch. 10, p. 102).
- For young women like Jane, educated but without high-born family connections, there were limited options in terms of making a living apart from being a governess – a dependent, in other words.
- Marriage was taken very seriously as a financial and business deal. Fathers gave their daughters dowries when they married.
- Girls such as Jane had few options open to them apart from using their education as a marketable resource.

In the novel, Charlotte Brontë introduces several strong female characters who all have to deal with their lack of independence.

- Miss Temple, Diana and Mary Rivers all possess the values Jane admires. They all have to work for a living for rather meagre wages and therefore have little independence.
- They all marry men who deserve them and whom they love, rather than settling for financial security at the expense of happiness.
- Jane is very conscious that these women are not treated as they deserve to be: note the description of Miss Temple's reaction to being admonished by Mr Brocklehurst – 'she now gazed straight before her, and her face, naturally pale as marble, appeared to be assuming also the coldness and fixity of that material' (Ch. 7, p. 75).
- Jane hates the thought of Diana and Mary wasting their talents as governesses: 'by whose wealthy and haughty members they were regarded only as humble dependents, and who neither knew nor sought one of their innate excellences' (Ch. 30, p. 405).

KEY QUOTATION: JANE'S CHARACTER **A01**

Throughout her life Jane is placed in situations where she is dependent on others. She learns to keep her passionate and assertive side quiet except when driven to extremes: 'I never in my life have known any medium in my dealings with positive, hard characters, antagonistic to my own, between absolute submission and determined revolt' (Ch. 34, p. 462). Nonetheless, she is an assertive heroine. Look at the confidence and eloquence in her dialogues with Rochester from the start of their relationship. She is neither meek nor subservient with anyone; she often chooses to keep quiet rather than speak her mind unguardedly, but when called upon she is forthright and powerfully honest in her opinions.

AIMING HIGH: WRITING ABOUT JANE

Think about the circumstances surrounding Jane's eventual marriage to Rochester. He is now legally 'free' to marry her, but there are other possible factors which make their marriage more comfortable for the reader. Jane is now financially independent with a fortune of her own. Also, some critics have noted that Rochester is physically more dependent on Jane now, which could further reinforce the equal status between them.

SOCIAL STATUS

Class divisions and social status were more fixed and pronounced in the nineteenth century than they are today. The idea that high social status does not necessarily mean goodness is an important theme:

- Jane is very conscious that, socially, she is inferior to many of those with whom she associates in spite of being educated, and that money dictates where one fits on the social ladder.

- The idea of respect being earned and not deserved due to one's bank balance is important to our appreciation of Jane. She attaches little value to wealth and does not see it as the road to any kind of happy life.

- For example, she comments on the prospective marriage between Rochester and Blanche: 'I saw he was going to marry her, for family, perhaps political reasons because her rank and connections suited him; I felt he had not given her his love, and that her qualifications were ill-adapted to win from him that treasure' (Ch. 18, p. 216). She, on the other hand, is 'poor, obscure, plain, and little' (Ch. 23, p. 292).

- Societal forms and conventions were much more strictly adhered to in the nineteenth century than they are today.

- This attitude is also shown by Mrs Fairfax: 'Equality of position and fortune is often advisable in such cases' (Ch. 24, p. 305).

- Jane's mother is cast off by her family for marrying someone from an 'inferior' class to herself.

KEY CONTEXT **A03**

Bertha Rochester has sometimes been interpreted as a symbol of how women of that time and society were repressed and denied the opportunity to express their feelings. Many feminist interpretations of *Jane Eyre* have leapt to the defence of Bertha and used her to pronounce harsh judgement on Rochester. We never know if his account of their marriage and early years is true; we are only given one side of the story.

THEME TRACKER **A01**

Social status

- Chapter 1: Charlotte Brontë introduces Jane's unequal status and lack of power.

- Chapter 18: Jane's social status as governess is mocked by Blanche Ingram.

- Chapter 23: Jane defends her right to be seen as equal.

CONTEXTS

MARRIAGE AND MONEY

At the time that Charlotte Brontë wrote *Jane Eyre*, female independence was often achieved through financial security. For women of Brontë's class, with no money of their own, marriage was the route to this financial security. For high-born women, this meant staying in the family home until a suitable marriage came along. Marriage was commonly seen as a way of securing and growing the family fortune – more of a business arrangement than a romantic one. The family of a young lady would offer a dowry in the event of her marriage. A young lady would be expected to learn a range of accomplishments, including embroidery, the piano and languages, until such time that a suitable match could be found for her.

Blanche Ingram is typical of this class of women; she sees a potential match with Rochester as a means of securing the family fortune and is easily discouraged when he hints that his fortune might be only 'a third of what was supposed' (Ch. 23, p. 294). This view of marriage as a practical arrangement can also be seen in St John Rivers' refusal to acknowledge his love for Rosamund Oliver and his proposal to Jane instead, believing that she will make a better missionary's wife.

KEY QUOTATION: JANE ON MARRIAGE (A01)

When Jane discovers that she is an heiress to a large fortune, St John suggests that this brings with it the opportunity to marry. Jane rejects this quite violently: 'No one would take me for love; and I will not be regarded in the light of a mere money speculation. And I do not want a stranger – unsympathising, alien, different from me; I want my kindred' (Ch. 33, p. 447). This highlights how unusual Jane's feelings are in the context of attitudes towards marriage at that time.

GOVERNESSES

The role of governess was a staple in affluent nineteenth-century wealthy households. At this time there was no state education and local schools were few and far between. Some were set up by local religious leaders, like St John who runs his charity school for the sons of farm workers in the neighbourhood. However, the more common scenario at the time was for children of the landed gentry to be educated at home until the young gentlemen were sent away to boarding school, leaving the young ladies to stay at home and be educated by a governess.

A governess was basically a servant in the household. She would teach basic English and maths along with some geography and history, French, and the approved social accomplishments such as the piano and fine sewing. Governesses generally came from families like the Brontës, the educated middle classes – girls with some education but no dowry and therefore not much prospect of marriage.

TOP TIP (A03)

Understanding the world of the writer, and of the novel, includes appreciating how the beliefs and attitudes of the characters would have been influenced and shaped by their society and their belief systems.

KEY CONTEXT (A03)

Like Jane, Charlotte Brontë was sent to a school where she eventually, like Jane and Miss Temple, became a teacher. As a young adult, Charlotte, like her sisters, worked for a time as a governess for a wealthy family.

KEY QUOTATION: GOVERNESSES A01

Jane calls the prospect of the role of governess 'A new servitude' (Ch. 10, p. 102). She recognises that the options open to her are extremely limited. Governesses were often seen as servants, hence Blanche Ingram has no compunction about describing 'half of them [as] detestable and the rest ridiculous' (Ch. 17, p. 205) in front of Jane herself.

RELIGION IN NINETEENTH-CENTURY ENGLAND

In the nineteenth century, England was a Christian country and religion played a vital role in daily life. Charlotte Brontë introduces three main figures into *Jane Eyre* to whom religion is important – Mr Brocklehurst, Helen Burns and St John Rivers. These three characters represent different aspects of Christianity, all of which Jane ultimately rejects in her search for how to lead a happy Christian life.

SETTINGS

THE WEATHER

There are numerous examples of climatic conditions intensifying mood in the novel (pathetic fallacy). The bleak view from the window in the opening section reinforces the idea of little Jane's unhappiness. The freezing conditions at Lowood add to the misery there in the same way that the storm in the Thornfield orchard on the night of Rochester's proposal creates a feeling of foreboding.

SURROUNDINGS

Houses and possessions are used to add information about characters. The Rivers are not wealthy and yet Jane approves of their home because it typifies the values of cleanliness and common sense. She is much more at home in this kind of environment than in the grand houses of Gateshead or Thornfield, and it is logical that she and Rochester should eventually settle at Ferndean Manor which is much less imposing than Thornfield Hall.

REVISION FOCUS: THE GOTHIC

Charlotte Brontë was very much influenced by writers of Gothic fiction, with its melodrama, haunted and gloomy castles, and innocent heroines. Thornfield is vaguely threatening with its sombre rooms hung with tapestry, its strange noises and mysterious secrets, and fits into this genre very well: 'I lingered in the long passage ... narrow, low, and dim, with only one little window at the far end ... like a corridor in some Bluebeard's castle' (Ch. 11, p. 126).

See how many other Gothic settings you can find in the novel.

KEY CONTEXT A03

Charlotte Brontë based Thornfield Hall on a real place she had visited as a governess. There are several opinions on where the 'real' Thornfield Hall is, however: Haddon Hall, North Lees Hall and High Sunderland Hall have all been suggested.

TOP TIP A03

The setting of *Jane Eyre* is vital to the plot and action, and often provides an added dimension which helps the reader's understanding of character and scene.

Gateshead Hall

Lowood School

Thornfield Hall

Ferndean Manor

Marsh End

Key

1 Gateshead to Lowood
2 Lowood to Thornfield
3 Thornfield to Gateshead
4 Gateshead to Thornfield
5 Thornfield to Marsh End
6 Marsh End to Thornfield
7 Thornfield to Ferndean

PROGRESS AND REVISION CHECK

SECTION ONE: CHECK YOUR KNOWLEDGE

Answer these quick questions to test your basic knowledge of the themes, contexts and settings of the novel:

1 Why does Mr Brocklehurst treat the pupils at Lowood so severely?

2 Why does Jane disapprove of Rochester marrying Blanche Ingram?

3 Why is Mrs Fairfax concerned about Rochester and Jane's marriage?

4 Why does Jane refuse to go to India with St John Rivers?

5 What happens to the chestnut tree that Jane and Rochester are standing by when he proposes to her?

6 Why does St John Rivers want to go to India?

7 What does Jane describe as 'A new servitude'?

8 Why does Jane refuse to stay with Mr Rochester when she finds out that he is married?

9 Who describes Jane as 'poor, obscure, plain, and little'?

10 Why does Helen Burns never complain about the way she is treated at school?

SECTION TWO: CHECK YOUR UNDERSTANDING

Here is a task which requires a slightly longer response. Try to write at least three or four paragraphs:

Task: The weather and the natural world is a strong influence in *Jane Eyre*. Write about:

- how Jane is affected by the weather and the natural world
- how Charlotte Brontë uses the weather and the natural world in the novel.

PROGRESS CHECK

GOOD PROGRESS

I can:

- explain the main themes, contexts and settings in the text and how they contribute to the effect on the reader ☐
- use a range of appropriate evidence to support any points I make about these elements. ☐

EXCELLENT PROGRESS

I can:

- analyse in detail the way themes are developed and presented across the novel ☐
- refer closely to key aspects of context and setting and the implications they have for the writer's viewpoint, and the interpretation of relationships and ideas. ☐

FORM

OVERVIEW

KEY CONTEXT (A03)

The novel as a form was growing in popularity during the early part of the nineteenth century. Novels that told the stories of ordinary people were still relatively new at this time, and one of the reasons for the enormous popularity of *Jane Eyre* was that it told the story of an ordinary member of society without rank or wealth.

The form of a text is the set of conventions that govern its overall shape. For example, a novel:

- is generally a lengthy prose fiction text
- is usually divided into chapters
- is usually organised chronologically
- usually spans a more lengthy period of time than a short story.

BILDUNGSROMAN

A Bildungsroman follows the journey of a child from naïve innocence through to adult maturity and wisdom. Along the way, the character learns from the experiences they have and the people they meet. Jane's metaphorical journey is shown through several literal journeys and destinations, where she meets more people and learns more things about herself and the world. Eventually, these journeys result in her becoming a fully rounded adult with self-knowledge and the peace that comes from being reconciled with who she is and how she wants to live her life.

KEY QUOTATION: JANE ON JOURNEYS (A01)

When Jane returns to Gateshead Hall, she says that 'I still felt as a wanderer on the face of the earth' (Ch 21, p. 262). This journey is half way through the novel and demonstrates that Jane has not yet completed her progress into adult maturity.

THE GOTHIC

Gothic fiction was popular as a genre in nineteenth-century fiction. Some of the common features include dark, mysterious stately homes or castles, a sense of mystery and looming danger, and a central female character who is alone and vulnerable. All of these features are used by Charlotte Brontë especially during the Thornfield Hall period of the novel.

AIMING HIGH: CHARLOTTE BRONTË'S USE OF ROMANTICISM

The influence of the Romantic movement can be seen in Charlotte Brontë's use of the weather as a powerful natural force. A popular theme in Romanticism is the relationship between humans and nature and how humanity could benefit and learn from this relationship. Another common theme in Romanticism is the voice of the 'common man'. This influence can be seen in *Jane Eyre* in terms of Jane learning to address her own misconceptions about the effects of poverty on the ability to live a decent, honest life.

STRUCTURE

OVERVIEW

The autobiographical form of *Jane Eyre* means that the novel follows a linear narrative. Jane's personal journey can also be said to have several stages, each with its own purpose:

- From childhood to maturity
- From restriction to freedom
- From unhappiness to happiness
- From innocence to knowledge

The idea of a journey through life is highlighted by the solitary journeys that Jane takes between the five main locations in the novel:

1. Gateshead Hall
2. Lowood School
3. Thornfield Hall
4. Marsh End/Moor House
5. Ferndean Manor

Note that Jane goes through severe tests at each stage, so that she eventually deserves her happiness. It is only when she reaches her destination that the journey is at an end – as marked by her settling at Ferndean Manor for life, her 'happy ending'. Although the novel covers the whole of Jane's life, only the most dramatic two years are dwelt upon in detail. The Thornfield section is the longest in spite of being the shortest period of time: seventeen chapters out of thirty-eight. This marks it as the most important phase of Jane's life, as well as the most interesting to the reader.

AIMING HIGH: THE NARRATOR

Notice the positioning of the narrator in terms of the events and the story of the novel. Jane Eyre tells her story ten years after the last event in the novel, her arrival in Ferndean. So it is written from the perspective of looking back on quite distant events in some cases. Think about what this adds to the novel, in particular the ways in which the narrator comments on the thoughts and behaviour of her younger self.

TOP TIP: WRITING ABOUT STRUCTURE (A02)

Think about the ways that Charlotte Brontë uses structure to develop the plot, the characters and the themes. Journeys are an important structural feature in *Jane Eyre*: when you are writing about the journeys, it is useful to think about the significance of each one and the extent to which they link to the overall themes and the development of character. In other words, what function does each journey, or journeys as a whole, serve in the overall novel? What does the reader learn about themes and character through the use of this structural technique?

TOP TIP (A02)

Considering why Charlotte Brontë used different locations in the novel might help to develop a better understanding of the craft of the writer. Think about why it is important for Jane to move from place to place, and what each of these journeys, destinations and circumstances adds to her understanding of herself, and to the reader's understanding of her.

LANGUAGE

OVERVIEW

A writer's style refers to the choices they make about the words they use, the way they organise and structure their ideas, and the effects they want to create. The resulting text is the end-product of a range of these choices. For example, in relation to *Jane Eyre*, think about how:

- The novel depicts a good woman who is capable of strong emotion and passion.

- Jane's first encounter with Mr Rochester establishes the ultimate pattern of their relationship, the wounded man tended by a devoted woman, but she is at pains to point out that beauty in masculine form is not important to her: 'I ... should have shunned [it] as one would fire, lightning, or anything else that is bright' (Ch. 12, p. 134).

- For all that, her description of him reveals the way she is stirred by his essential maleness: having noted his 'considerable breadth of chest', she observes his 'dark face, with stern features and a heavy brow' and comments finally that 'the roughness of the traveller set me at my ease' (Ch. 12, p. 134).

- Rochester, as the language reveals, clearly is a man capable of stirring this young woman's emotions and passions.

LANGUAGE DEVICE: AUTOBIOGRAPHY

What is an autobiography?	A non-fiction account of a life, told by the subject of the autobiography in the first person
Example	At the start of Chapter 10, Jane speaks directly to the reader as she introduces the next phase of her life: 'Hitherto I have recorded in detail the events of my insignificant existence: to the first ten years of my life I have given almost as many chapters. But this is not to be a regular autobiography.' (p. 99)
Effect	The effect of this device is to create a connection between the reader and the narrator of the story. Also, it highlights the social realism of *Jane Eyre* as opposed to the fashionable 'romance' novels that preceded the work of writers such as the Brontës and Jane Austen. It increases the sense that this story is that of an ordinary human being.

The facsimile of the frontispiece to the first edition of this novel reads: '*Jane Eyre*: an Autobiography, edited by Currer Bell'. The book is not, however, an autobiography but a work of fiction. And of course Jane Eyre is not a real person, but a character existing in a narrative. However, the novel is highly reminiscent of an autobiography. It is narrated in the first person, thereby immediately drawing the reader into a closer sense of identification with the central character, and implicitly creating more of a sense of realism.

TOP TIP (A02)

When referring to 'language', think about more than the effects of particular techniques such as similes and metaphors. Focus attention on the actual words themselves: the use of description, for example, or the selection of a particular word to highlight a theme, idea, feeling or aspect of a character.

Charlotte Brontë

TOP TIP: WRITING FROM A MODERN PERSPECTIVE (A03)

It is important to bear in mind that as twenty-first-century readers, we have knowledge about the author that was unknown to the contemporary readership. We know that many details of the work were drawn directly from Charlotte Brontë's personal experience. Many characters, situations and places are taken from her own life and the eponymous heroine bears, in many respects, a startling resemblance to Charlotte Brontë herself. Although not completely autobiographical, this novel is not completely fictional either.

LANGUAGE DEVICE: NARRATOR

What is a narrator?	The person telling the story to the reader, usually either in the first person such as in *Jane Eyre*, or in the third person as an omniscient narrator
Example	Jane constantly addresses her reader directly: 'Reader, I married him' (Ch. 38, p. 517).
Effect	This draws attention to the relationship between the reader and the narrator, which creates more empathy and engagement with Jane.

Charlotte Brontë draws attention to the fact that there is a narrator telling a story, but the reader is invited to believe it is real: 'whether what followed was the effect of excitement the reader shall judge' (Ch. 35, p. 483). To a certain extent Brontë was following literary convention by exploring the use of narrative stance in storytelling. For example, she often shifts between past and present tense for different effects. Brontë repeatedly highlights the fact that the novel is a narrative account: at the beginning of Chapter 11 she remarks, 'A new chapter in a novel is something like a new scene in a play.' (p. 111).

TOP TIP (A02)

Notice the moments when Jane's narration slips into the present tense. What might the effect be of this change? Think about what it suggests about Jane's feelings at that moment – might she not want the moment to end, or might she feel trapped in that moment? Chapter 17 provides a good example of this technique.

LANGUAGE DEVICE: IMAGERY AND SYMBOLISM

What are imagery and symbolism?	A device used to 'paint a picture' in the mind of the reader: similes, metaphors, personification are all examples of imagery. Symbolism is the use of objects or events to suggest particular meanings.
Example	When Rochester first proposes to Jane, a fierce storm ensues: 'the great horse-chestnut at the bottom of the orchard had been struck by lightning in the night, and half of it split away' (Ch. 23, p. 296).
Effect	This symbolises the 'split' between Jane and Rochester that will shortly follow and highlights the close connection between the characters and the natural world.

Imagery of fire and ice is used throughout the novel to represent Jane's internal battle between passion and reason. Rochester is twice attacked by Bertha, both times through fire. St John Rivers on the other hand is closely linked with snow and frost: 'the cloak that covered his tall figure [was] all white as a glacier' (Ch. 33, p. 435).

Names also have a symbolic function in *Jane Eyre*: 'Eyre', for example, came from a family called Eyre whose house had a room in it which had apparently housed a woman who was mentally unstable. The name also has resonance with the sense of being as 'free as air'. Rochester constantly refers to Jane as a creature of air: a fairy, elf or sprite, as if there is an other-worldliness to her.

A further image is the dream of the 'little child' (Ch. 25, p. 324) that Jane struggles to protect. Bessie comments early in the novel that 'to dream of children was a sure sign of trouble' (Ch. 21, p. 254). Dreams are very symbolic in *Jane Eyre*, possibly suggesting the power of Jane's interior life and its inability to find expression in reality.

AIMING HIGH: IMAGERY OF FIRE

The fire at Thornfield, and Rochester's actions, have a symbolic function as well as a dramatic effect on the plot. Rochester is portrayed as a man of fiery emotions and passions. Fire is often thought to have a cleansing function, and therefore his selfless actions in the fire could be interpreted as ridding him of his sins and cleansing his soul. What he does is admirable and shows him to be a good and decent human being who puts the welfare of others above that of himself. The fire could also be seen as a punishment for his previous immoral behaviour, however: he loses his sight and one of his hands in the fire.

PROGRESS AND REVISION CHECK

SECTION ONE: CHECK YOUR KNOWLEDGE

Answer these quick questions to test your basic knowledge of the form, structure and language of the novel:

1. Who is the narrator of *Jane Eyre*?

2. What does Charlotte Brontë use as an image of danger ahead in Chapter 23?

3. In how many different places does Jane live during the novel?

4. What does 'chronological' mean?

5. Who are the two characters associated with imagery of fire and imagery of ice?

6. Who does Rochester describe as a 'mocking changeling'?

7. What does Jane tell Rochester she has dreamed about having to look after?

8. Is the novel written mostly in the past tense or present tense?

9. Is the novel narrated from a first person or third person perspective?

10. Is Jane an omniscient narrator?

SECTION TWO: CHECK YOUR UNDERSTANDING

Here is a task which requires a slightly longer response. Try to write at least three or four paragraphs:

Task: *Jane Eyre* is a Bildungsroman or 'education novel'. During the course of the novel, Jane develops into a mature adult. Write about:

- what Jane learns about life and herself during the course of the novel
- how Charlotte Brontë uses different locations and characters to convey Jane's development into a mature adult.

PROGRESS CHECK

GOOD PROGRESS

I can:

- explain how the writer uses form, structure and language to develop the action, show relationships and develop ideas ☐
- use relevant quotations to support the points I make, and make reference to the effect of some language choices. ☐

EXCELLENT PROGRESS

I can:

- analyse in detail Charlotte Brontë's use of particular forms, structures and language techniques, to convey ideas, create characters and evoke mood or setting ☐
- select from a range of evidence, including apt quotations, to infer the effect of particular language choices, and to develop wider interpretations. ☐

UNDERSTANDING THE QUESTION

For your exam, you will be answering an extract-based question and/or a question on the whole of *Jane Eyre*. Check with your teacher to see what sort of question you are doing. Whatever the task, questions in exams will need **decoding**. This means highlighting and understanding the key words so that the answer you write is relevant.

BREAK DOWN THE QUESTION

Pick out the **key words** or phrases. For example:

Read from 'I grieve to leave Thornfield' to 'equal – as we are!'
(Ch. 23, p. 292)

Question: How does Charlotte Brontë **present** Jane as a **strong female character** in this **extract** and in the novel **as a whole**?

What does this tell you?

- Focus on **the idea of 'strong'** in terms of Jane in the context of this passage and the novel as a whole.
- The word **'present'** tells you that you should focus on the ways Brontë reveals these ideas about Jane.
- The phrases 'this extract' and 'novel as a whole' mean you need to **start** with the given **extract** and then **widen your discussion** to the rest of the novel, whilst sticking to the same question focus **in both**.

TOP TIP (A01)

You might also be asked to 'refer closely to', which means picking out specific examples from the text, or to focus on 'methods and techniques', which means the 'things' Brontë does, for example, the use of a particular dramatic device, a change of mood, etc.

PLANNING YOUR ANSWER

It is vital that you generate ideas quickly and plan your answer efficiently when you sit the exam. Stick to your plan and, with a watch at your side, tick off each part as you progress.

STAGE 1: GENERATE IDEAS QUICKLY

Briefly **list your key ideas** based on the question you have **decoded.** For example:

In the extract:

- *Jane is honest about her feelings.*
- *Jane takes over the conversation and speaks much more than Rochester.*
- *Examples of passionate language show how strongly Jane feels.*

In the novel as a whole:

- *Jane's social position makes her relatively weak.*
- *As a child, Jane speaks her mind even when she has no power.*
- *Jane is determined to lead the life she wants and to be independent.*

STAGE 2: JOT DOWN USEFUL QUOTATIONS (OR KEY EVENTS)

For example, from the extract: *'Do you think because I am poor, obscure, plain, and little'* (Ch. 23, p. 292)

From the novel as a whole: *'How dare I? Because it is the truth.'* (Ch. 4, p. 44)

STAGE 3: PLAN FOR PARAGRAPHS

Use paragraphs to plan your answer. For example:

Paragraph	Point
Paragraph 1	**Introduce** the **argument** you wish to make: *In this extract and in the novel as a whole, Charlotte Brontë presents Jane as a strong female character. She is strong in terms of her role as the central character and narrator, and also in terms of the world she lives in.*
Paragraph 2	Your first point: *In the extract Jane shows herself to be very strong. She speaks honestly and passionately to Rochester about how she feels and demonstrates a clear understanding of her place in the world and how unfair it is that she should be so powerless.*
Paragraph 3	Your second point: *Brontë highlights this strength in terms of the ways Jane speaks to Rochester in this extract. Her language is full of passionate words and she uses exclamation marks to indicate the strength of her feelings. She is not afraid to make her feelings clear.*
Paragraph 4	Your third point: *The reader already knows that Jane is capable of voicing very strongly held opinions. For example her argument with Mrs Reed earlier in the novel shows that she is prepared to stand up for herself and for what she believes is right.*
Paragraph 5	Your fifth point: *This strength of character is further demonstrated in the way that Jane leaves Rochester even though it breaks her heart to do so. She does this because her conscience and her sense of morality are stronger than her desire for happiness at this point in the novel.* [You may want to add further paragraphs if you have time.]
Conclusion	**Sum up** your argument: *Jane is a strong, or important, character to the reader because she is the protagonist of 'Jane Eyre' and therefore the reader is focused on her story. However, she is also strong in terms of the qualities she demonstrates and her determination to stick by her principles in spite of the circumstances she finds herself in.*

TOP TIP (A02)

When discussing Charlotte Brontë's language, make sure you refer to the techniques she uses, and, most importantly, the *effect* of those techniques. Don't just write: *Charlotte Brontë uses lots of exclamation marks here*, write: *Charlotte Brontë's use of exclamation marks shows/demonstrates/conveys the ideas that ...*

RESPONDING TO WRITERS' EFFECTS

The two most important assessment objectives are **AO1** and **AO2**. They are about *what* writers do (the choices they make, and the effects these create), *what* your ideas are (your analysis and interpretation), and *how* you write about them (how well you explain your ideas).

ASSESSMENT OBJECTIVE 1

What does it say?	What does it mean?	Dos and don'ts
Read, understand and respond to texts. Students should be able to: ● Maintain a critical style and develop an informed personal response ● Use textual references, including quotations, to support and illustrate interpretations	You must: ● Use some of the literary terms you have learned (correctly!) ● Write in a professional way (not a sloppy, chatty way) ● Show you have thought for yourself ● Back up your ideas with examples, including quotations	**Don't write …** *Jane is a strong character. Charlotte Brontë uses lots of words that shows that she is strong. She says 'you are passionate' in Chapter 4.* **Do write …** *Charlotte Brontë presents Jane as a strong, determined character, for example in her exchange with Mrs Reed where she is criticised for being 'passionate'. Brontë's use of the adjective suggests that the young Jane must learn to hide her feelings in order to gain the approval of others.*

IMPROVING YOUR CRITICAL STYLE

Use a variety of words and phrases to show effects. For example:

Charlotte Brontë *suggests …, conveys …, implies …, presents how …, explores …, demonstrates …, describes how …, shows how …*

I/we (as readers) *infer …, recognise …, understand …, question …, see …, are given …, reflect …*

For example, look at these two alternative paragraphs by different students about Jane. Note the difference in the quality of expression.

Student A:

> This sounds as if Charlotte Brontë is speaking

> This is a bit descriptive

Charlotte Brontë says that Jane is very angry and cross when she talks to Mrs Reed when they have the argument in Chapter 4. She says 'I am glad you are no relation of mine'. This shows that she is brave because she stands up to Mrs Reed and is very rude to her. This shows that Jane is a passionate character and brave because she is standing up to an adult.

> This is one possible interpretation but there are others as well

> Seems to be repeating the same ideas

> Not really explaining much about Jane or her relationship with Mrs Reed

Student B:

| Focus on what the writer is doing |
| Good use of embedded evidence |
| Considering more than one interpretation |

Charlotte Brontë presents Jane as a strong character in Chapter 4 where she confronts Mrs Reed for the last time as a child. She highlights Jane's strength of character with the bravery with which she asserts that she 'dares' to speak out 'because it is the truth'. She describes Mrs Reed as 'bad, hard-hearted' which not only demonstrates her ability to stand up to an authority figure but also seems to suggest that she is already a good judge of character.

| 'confronts' is a good choice of word as it accurately expresses the situation |
| Using 'seems to suggest' indicates that the student is thinking and weighing up more subtle meanings |

ASSESSMENT OBJECTIVE 2

What does it say?	What does it mean?	Dos and don'ts
Analyse the language, form and structure used by a writer to create meanings and effects, using relevant subject terminology where appropriate.	'Analyse' – comment **in detail** on **particular aspects** of the text or language 'language' – vocabulary, imagery, variety of sentences, dialogue/speech, etc. 'form' – **how** the story is told (e.g. first person narrative, letters, diaries, chapter by chapter?) 'structure' – the **order** in which events are revealed, or in which characters appear, or descriptions are presented 'create meanings' – what can we, as readers, **infer** from what the writer tells us? What is **implied** by particular descriptions, or events? 'subject terminology' – **words** you should use when **writing** about novels, such as 'character', 'protagonist', 'imagery', 'setting', etc.	**Don't write:** The opening of the novel is really good because it describes what Jane can see and sets the scene for the reader. **Do write:** Charlotte Brontë highlights Jane's isolation and misery with the use of weather symbolism in the first chapter of the novel: the 'drear November day' suggests a dark mood, reinforced with 'pale blank mist and cloud', not only intensifying the gloomy tone but also linking to Jane's circumstances at Gateshead.

THE THREE 'I'S

- The best analysis focuses on specific ideas, events or uses of language and thinks about what is **implied**.
- This means drawing **inferences**. On the surface, Jane standing up to Mrs Reed when she is a child shows us that she is strong-willed and not afraid to say what she thinks – but what deeper ideas might it signify about her character, her bravery and her principles?
- From the inferences you make across the text as a whole, you can arrive at your own **interpretation** – a sense of the bigger picture, a wider evaluation of a person, relationship or idea.

USING QUOTATIONS

One of the secrets of success in writing exam essays is to use quotations **effectively**. There are five basic principles:

1. Only quote what is most useful.
2. Do not use a quotation that repeats what you have just written.
3. Put quotation marks, e.g. ' ', around the quotation.
4. Write the quotation exactly as it appears in the original.
5. Use the quotation so that it fits neatly into your sentence.

EXAM FOCUS: USING QUOTATIONS (A01)

Quotations should be used to develop the line of thought in your essay, and 'zoom in' on key details such as language choices. The example below shows a clear and effective way of doing this:

Point → Charlotte Brontë presents Rochester as someone determined to fight for happiness. In Chapter 23, he says, 'For man's opinion – I defy it'. ← **Quotation**

Explanation/effect → This suggests that he knows that what he is doing is wrong but is so desperate to be married to Jane that he is going to proceed anyway.

However, really **high-level responses** will go further. They will make an even more precise point, support it with an even more appropriate quotation, focus in on particular words and phrases and explain the effect or what is implied to make a wider point or draw inferences. Here is an example:

Strong point → Charlotte Brontë presents Rochester as full of grim and dark determination, full of 'strong workings' and 'strange gleams'. ← **Effective use of embedded evidence**

Second good use of evidence → His warning: 'man meddle not with me: I have her, and will hold her' highlights his fear that he will not in fact be able to 'hold' Jane, and the modal verb 'will' demonstrates how strongly he feels and ← **Appropriate use of technical terminology**

Focuses in closely on selected word → how desperate he is to be certain of the prospect of marrying Jane, as well as implying his insecurity. ← **Language analysis**

SPELLING, PUNCTUATION AND GRAMMAR

SPELLING

Remember to spell correctly the **author's** name, the names of all the **characters**, and the names of **places**.

It is a good idea to list some of the key spellings you know you sometimes get wrong *before* the exam starts. Then use it to check as you go along. Sometimes it is easy to make small errors as you write but if you have your key word list nearby you can check against it.

PUNCTUATION

Remember:

- Use **full stops and commas in sentences accurately to make clear points**. Don't write long, rambling sentences that don't make sense; equally, avoid using a lot of short repetitive ones. Write in a fluent way, using linking words and phrases, and use **inverted commas** for **quotations**:

Don't write	Do write
Jane and Rochester have a lot in common through the book and right from the start they seem to be on the same wavelength and they have lots of conversations that they both enjoy where they want to judge each other for themselves.	Jane and Rochester appear to have a lot in common, although they come from different worlds. From the start of the novel they seem to be on the same wavelength, having lots of conversations which they seem to enjoy. They are both keen to 'judge' each other for themselves.

GRAMMAR

When you are writing about the text, make sure you:

- Use the present tense for discussing what the writer does
- Use pronouns and references back to make your writing flow:

Don't write	Do write
Whilst St John seems to be motivated by religious beliefs, St John's coldness and determination made St John seem harsh and unsympathetic.	Whilst St John seems to be motivated by religious beliefs, **his** coldness and determination **make him** seem harsh and unsympathetic.

TOP TIP A04

Remember that spelling, punctuation and grammar is worth approximately **5%** of your overall marks, which could mean the difference between one grade and another.

TOP TIP A04

Practise your spellings of key literature terms you might use when writing about the text such as: ironic, omniscient (narrator), simile, metaphor, imagery, protagonist, character, theme, hierarchy, etc.

TOP TIP A04

Enliven your essay by varying the way your sentences begin. For example: *Jane finds herself drawn to Rochester, despite their difference in age, status and life experience* can also be written as: *Despite their difference in age, status and life experience, Jane finds herself drawn to Rochester.*

ANNOTATED SAMPLE ANSWERS

This section provides three **sample responses**, one at **mid** level, one at a **good level** and one at a **very high level**.

> **Question**: In this extract, Jane meets Rochester for the first time.
>
> **Read from**: 'Something of daylight still lingered' to 'till I see you are fit to mount your horse.' (Ch. 12, p. 134)
>
> Write about Charlotte Brontë's presentation of Rochester.
> - How is he presented through Jane's first impressions of him here?
> - How is he presented elsewhere in the novel?

SAMPLE ANSWER 1

A01 Comment on the significance of the moment in the novel

In this passage Jane meets Mr Rochester for the first time. As he rides past her on a country lane, his horse stumbles and he falls from it. This is important to the novel as it shows that in Jane's presence Mr Rochester can be weaker than he would like to be.

A01 Rather simple comment on the quotation

A01 Fair point but rather descriptive

When Jane looks at him and describes him she says that he seems dark and angry. 'He had a dark face, with stern features and a heavy brow; his eyes and gathered eyebrows looked ireful and thwarted just now'. This suggests that Rochester is an angry man and also that he is not that attractive. Jane is not frightened that he looks 'ireful' though and carries on looking at him, which shows that she is interested in him and might be attracted to him.

A01 Quite a long quotation

A01 Sound embedded quotation

A01 Clear comment on effect of evidence

Rochester is not polite to Jane. It says that he is rude to her; 'the frown, the roughness'. This shows that Mr Rochester is not a polite person generally even when he is talking to a woman who he has never seen before. This might be because he has fallen from his horse so is shocked or hurt, but it also shows that he is usually not very polite or gentle in the way he speaks to people.

Jane is not frightened of him because he is not like a gentleman and isn't handsome. She describes his face having 'stern features and a heavy brow' but isn't put off by this because she would have felt more shy around someone handsome. This is because Jane doesn't have much experience of meeting men as she has been at an all girls' school all her life.

A01 Fair point but not that relevant to the task

In the rest of the book Brontë presents Mr Rochester as a powerful man and very unhappy. He spends a lot of time away from home and this is because he is trying to forget the burden of his wife Bertha. However, he does look after her even though he is unhappy and was tricked into marrying her by his family. He doesn't have her shut away in an institution and this shows that he takes his responsibilities seriously.

A01 Showing knowledge of the novel as a whole

A01 Evidence of knowledge of the novel as a whole but rather descriptive again and lacking detail

When Rochester falls in love with Jane, Brontë shows that he is sensitive and intelligent. Jane doesn't realise at first that he is in love with her but Brontë shows the reader that he has strong feelings for Jane, such as the night of the fire when Jane saves him and he doesn't want her to leave him. It is also shown when Jane asks to go back to see her aunt and Rochester doesn't want to let her go.

A01 Comment on the writer

A01 Focus back on the task as a whole

Therefore this extract shows that Rochester has a dark side and is not like a typical gentleman of the time. He is not particularly handsome and isn't particularly polite. However, Jane sees through all this and feels a connection to him right from the start.

A03 Attempt at contextual comment, needs developing

MID LEVEL

Comment

This is a clear response that makes some good points. They tend to be rather undeveloped and there is not much focus on the methods the writer uses. There is a tendency towards re-telling the story rather than focusing on the task. Some evidence is used well although one quotation in particular is unnecessarily long.

For a Good Level:

- More focus on language and techniques
- More detail on how Brontë presents Rochester in this extract and elsewhere in the novel
- More precise use of embedded evidence

SAMPLE ANSWER 2

A02 Focus on the writer

A01 Clear embedded quotation

A02 Rather straightforward comment on the effect of particular word choices

A01 Good point but not particularly relevant to an essay on Rochester

A01 Good link to previous paragraph

A03 Shows understanding of relative status and male/female relationships

A02 Clear explanation of metaphorical significance

A01 Linking the extract to the novel as a whole

A01 Good use of qualifying language

A02 Focus on the writer's use of description

A01 Shows knowledge of the rest of the novel

Brontë uses the first description of Rochester to present him to the reader as well as to Jane. Jane says 'I could see him plainly' which could be seen as a metaphor for how Jane 'sees' or understands and relates to Rochester throughout the novel. However, it is dark, which is also symbolic of Rochester's 'dark face' and also dark personality with secrets and mystery. This links to the fact that he does have a dark secret and is unhappy in his life. He also has 'stern features and a heavy brow' and his eyes are described as 'ireful and thwarted'. This makes him sound dangerous, gloomy and threatening. The effect of this might suggest that he is frightening to Jane, but instead she says that if he was handsome she would 'instinctively' know to 'shun' him, which suggests that her instincts draw her to him instead.

This extract introduces Rochester to the reader, but also introduces the relationship between Jane and Rochester. Jane isn't frightened or intimidated by him at all, which shows that she is quite a strong character. She describes him by saying he has a 'frown' and 'roughness' which introduce him as quite a gloomy character. This is important as Brontë is using the first description to tell the reader some important features about Rochester, and using the physical description of him to highlight some aspects of his personality.

He is also shown to be like this when Jane meets him next at Thornfield Hall and he questions her about her past and her abilities. He also speaks with 'roughness' to her here as well. Jane is not intimidated or frightened by this at all, and it shows that she understands Rochester well and that there is a connection between them. He is like her in the way that neither of them are comfortable in polite society and both of them speak plainly and honestly. This is one of the things that draws them to each other.

A01 Another good link to previous paragraph

A01 Useful direct quotation from the novel as a whole

A02 Plot points that show knowledge of the whole novel and also related to how Brontë demonstrates Rochester's character

A02 Focus on the purpose of the extract

A01 Relevant comments but straying into description of plot

A01 Conclusion that relates back to the task

This first meeting sets up this connection because Jane seems to see through the surface appearance of Rochester. It also sets up the equality of the relationship between them and shows that they will be equal in intelligence as well as having 'kindred' minds, as Jane puts it. As the novel progresses, Rochester is shown to be like this first description of him in many ways. Mrs Fairfax tells Jane that he is 'troubled' because of some family circumstances and spends lots of time abroad. This suggests that he is unhappy and unsettled. He is also shown to be lonely by the way he keeps the house locked up most of the time and doesn't socialise much.

However, Brontë also shows that Rochester is deep feeling and very passionate. He is shown to be a very sympathetic character by the way he feels about Jane and also by the way he sees through Blanche Ingram and also saves his servants from the fire at Thornfield. Also, he tries hard to save Bertha in spite of the fact that she is making his life miserable.

Overall, this extract introduces the character of Rochester through the language Brontë uses to describe him, and highlights some of the features of his personality that will be developed later in the novel.

GOOD LEVEL

Comment
This is quite a developed response in terms of the extract, although it has a tendency to slip into description in some places when referring to the novel as a whole. The focus on effects of language use are well developed overall and closely linked to the writer's purpose and meanings. There is some effective use of embedded evidence to support points. The style is appropriate to this type of essay.

For a High Level:
- More analysis of effects of particular word choices
- Focus on deeper meanings
- More developed analytical language

SAMPLE ANSWER 3

A02 Good reference to the use of setting

A02 Starting to analyse the evidence in more detail

A02 Detailed analysis of metaphor here

A03 Shows understanding of their relative status

A01 Key quotation from later in the novel, used effectively to support the ideas being explored

A01 Good use of embedded evidence

A02 Well-developed analysis of the effects of language

A02 Reference to technical terminology, appropriately used

A01 Developing an overview of the extract linked to the novel as a whole

A03 Starting to refer to contextual elements

This first description of Rochester is used by Brontë to introduce some important information about him, and about his relationship with Jane. The first sentence uses the setting to hint at a change: the 'daylight still lingered' as if night is on the way, possibly highlighting the change that is about to come in Jane's life through meeting Rochester. Not only is 'daylight' still lingering but 'the moon was waxing bright', which reinforces the idea of brightness that he will bring to her life. This contrasts with the references to Rochester's 'darkness' later in the passage and possibly suggests that there is a mixture of dark and light in the effect of the relationship on Jane, as well as a 'darkness' to Rochester's mind and soul. The 'waxing' of the moon relates to natural forces, as the moon is known to have influence over the tides. Brontë is possibly suggesting that the relationship between Jane and Rochester is an elemental force and linked to the powerful forces of the natural world. It could also hint at the force he has over her, as if it is also something natural and elemental.

When Jane says that 'I could see him plainly', this has a metaphorical as well as literal meaning. Jane 'sees' Rochester for the man that he is; she is not worldly-wise enough to be swayed or captivated by 'beauty, elegance, gallantry' but instead 'sees' the true character of Rochester the man. This central idea, of Jane being able to look beyond the superficial and grasp the essence of who Rochester is, is further developed as the novel progresses. This is one of the reasons he falls for her, and reflects his own capacity to see the 'real' Jane, 'equal as we are'.

This first description of Rochester gives an unconventional view of a romantic hero. He 'had a dark face, with stern features and a heavy brow' – the darkness and the heaviness all hinting towards a troubled mind and of someone carrying a heavy burden, which of course is shown to be true with the

A01 Further evidence of knowledge of the novel as a whole

A03 Demonstrating some insight into literary context

A01 Exploring the ideas in detail now

A01 Developing and exploring the idea in more detail, supported with precise reference to detail

A01 Analysis of particular details from the extract

A01 Very clear understanding of the major theme of the novel

A01 Summative point to reiterate main ideas in the response

revelations of his 'living wife' and the part that his family have played in his misery. The fact that he doesn't smile at Jane shows someone who has little use for common courtesies or 'gallantry', which is again highlighted by his manner to Jane when he meets her later and questions her about her life. Brontë's depiction of Rochester is very much in the style of the 'Byronic' hero and demonstrates the influence of Romantic ideas about passion: dark, troubled and potentially dangerous, rather than conventionally handsome, light-hearted and courteous. This isn't a conventional romance in many ways; Rochester is only seen as attractive as a potential husband for Blanche Ingram due to her perception of his wealth and she quickly decides not to marry him when he implies that this might be less than she thought. Although Rochester can play the role of 'gallant' man of society, Jane sees this as false and recognises that he has an 'absence of passion' towards Blanche. On the other hand, Rochester and Jane are completely suited to each other in much more important ways than social status or physical appearance. When Rochester talks about the 'cord of communion' between them, Brontë is referring to the emotional and spiritual connection that is shown to be far more important than financial wealth or physical beauty.

To sum up, in this first description, Brontë highlights many of the aspects of Rochester, and of Jane's relationship with Rochester, that underpin their relationship and the themes of equality and true love that are explored in 'Jane Eyre'.

VERY HIGH LEVEL

Comment
A detailed analysis of some precisely selected moments from the extract, showing strong engagement with the ideas that are highlighted. The style is appropriate and evidence is used skilfully to support points being made. There is some confident analysis of effects of language choices linked to themes and ideas.

PRACTICE TASK

Write a full-length response to this exam-style question and then use the **Mark scheme** on page 96 to assess your own response.

> **Question**: In Chapter 17, Jane watches a conversation between Blanche Ingram and Mr Rochester.
>
> Read from: '"Oh, I am so sick of the young men of the present day!"' to '"I am all obedience," was the response.' (Ch. 17, p. 208)
>
> How does Charlotte Brontë present Blanche Ingram?
>
> Write about:
>
> - How Brontë presents Blanche in this extract
> - How Brontë presents Blanche in the novel as a whole

Remember:

- Plan quickly and efficiently by using key words from the question.
- Write equally about the extract and the rest of the novel.
- Focus on the techniques Brontë uses and the effect of these on the reader.
- Support your ideas with relevant evidence, including quotations.

FURTHER QUESTIONS

1 In Chapter 12 Jane meets Rochester for the first time.

Read from: 'Something of daylight still lingered' to 'anything else that is bright but antipathetic' (Ch. 12, p. 134).

How does Charlotte Brontë present Jane's feelings for Rochester?

Write about:

- How Jane's feelings for Rochester are presented in this extract
- How Jane's feelings for Rochester are presented in the novel as a whole

2 'St John Rivers is a selfish, dominating man.' Explore the extent to which you agree with this view of St John Rivers.

Explore the ways in which Charlotte Brontë presents ideas about religion in *Jane Eyre*.

Consider:

- The importance of religion to Jane and some of the other characters
- How Brontë presents different ideas about religion in the novel

LITERARY TERMS

Bildungsroman	coming of age or 'education' novel
Byronic	a term referring to Lord Byron, used to describe a type of hero of Romantic literature: dark, brooding and dangerous
chronological	a style of narrative where the events are ordered in time sequence
context	the circumstances, surroundings, etc. that influence a text
dialogue	the speech or conversation of characters
eponymous	the person whose name is used as the title of the book
first person narrative	a story told from the point of view of the central character, using 'I'
genre	a 'kind' or 'type' of literature
Gothic	a story of cruel passions and supernatural terrors, usually in a medieval setting
image	mental picture created with words
imagery	figurative language including metaphors and similes
irony	the use of words to convey the opposite of their literal meaning; incongruity between what might be expected and what actually occurs
linear	similar to chronological – following a straightforward sequence of events
metaphor	a descriptive device which states that one thing is another, figuratively rather than literally
narrative	the story
narrative perspective	the point of view of the person telling the story
narrator	the person telling the story, may be involved or impartial to the story
omniscient	literally all-knowing – a type of narrator who knows more about the story than the characters
pathetic fallacy	a way of emphasising mood by linking it to the surrounding world
pathos	moments which evoke strong feelings of pity or sadness
personification	attributing human characteristics to an object or animal
plot device	any content that moves the plot of the story forward or affects its direction
present tense	writing as if experiencing events at that very moment
prose	writing not in verse or any other kind of structure
Romantic movement	a literary movement of the early nineteenth century that focused on emotions and the imagination
setting	the place or surroundings where a text takes place
simile	a form of imagery where one thing is compared to another, usually using 'as' or 'like'
subtext	the situation that lies behind the characters or events which may never be directly referred to
symbol	something used to represent something else, such as the weather, or colours
theme	the central ideas of the novel rather than merely the plot

CHECKPOINT ANSWERS

CHECKPOINT 1, page 13

He is concerned about her misery, identifies the cause of her depression and suggests that she is sent away to school.

CHECKPOINT 2, page 16

A feeling that she is isolated creates sympathy for the character.

CHECKPOINT 3, page 17

It adds to the impression we form of the harsh conditions endured by the girls at Lowood.

CHECKPOINT 4, page 18

They appear straight after Mr Brocklehurst's long speech about the value of restraint and suffering.

CHECKPOINT 5, page 24

She studies him closely and presents a detailed depiction of his looks and behaviour.

CHECKPOINT 6, page 27

She thinks about him all the time and is disappointed when she learns that he has left Thornfield.

CHECKPOINT 7, page 29

Charades, like Rochester dressing up as a fortune-teller, link to the theme of secrets, hidden truths and characters not behaving as they really are.

CHECKPOINT 8, page 31

Where the other women react hysterically, Jane is resourceful and measured in her response.

CHECKPOINT 9, page 33

She finally realises that she is deeply in love with Rochester yet is able to accept the pain she will feel when he marries another woman.

CHECKPOINT 10, page 36

You would have expected her to enjoy having him spend money on her but she feels the need to be independent and writes to her uncle for financial help.

CHECKPOINT 11, page 37

Quite simply, she trusts him and wants to believe in him.

CHECKPOINT 12, page 39

He loves her and she loves him but she cannot bring herself to act in a way that is morally wrong.

CHECKPOINT 13, page 41

The candle may be seen as a sign of hope: it may be tiny and it may be flickering but it represents the possibility of help and safety.

CHECKPOINT 14, page 41

It shows a delicacy and respect for privacy which Jane certainly empathises with.

CHECKPOINT 15, page 42

Money is often used as a dramatic device to assist plot resolution. Jane's determination to share the inheritance demonstrates that for her, family is much more important than financial wealth.

CHECKPOINT 16, page 43

It may not have replaced the life she wanted as the wife of Rochester but at least she feels she is doing the right thing.

CHECKPOINT 17, page 44

She enables us to see the extent to which St John Rivers will sacrifice personal happiness for a higher cause.

CHECKPOINT 18, page 45

Her ready generosity is another example of her exemplary fairness and sense of moral justice.

CHECKPOINT 19, page 49

He has paid for his past transgressions, so the partial regaining of sight signals a sort of forgiveness. He is also thereby empowered to become a better father and husband since he can see his infant son and fully express his love for Jane as mother of his child.

PROGRESS AND REVISION CHECK ANSWERS

PART TWO, pages 51–2

SECTION ONE: CHECK YOUR KNOWLEDGE

1. Bessie
2. Mr Lloyd
3. Miss Temple
4. Helen Burns
5. Nobody, she does it alone
6. French
7. The horse slips on the ice
8. Her painting ability
9. Blanche Ingram
10. A fortune-teller
11. Bertha Rochester
12. Richard Mason
13. She is dying and wishes to clear her conscience
14. Her Christian morality is more important to her than her earthly happiness
15. St John, Diana and Mary Rivers
16. A missionary
17. Rosamund Oliver
18. She divides it between herself and the Rivers cousins
19. She imagines she can hear him calling to her
20. Bertha Rochester burns it to the ground

SECTION TWO: CHECK YOUR UNDERSTANDING

Task 1

- Rochester has a dominating character: 'Excuse my tone of command; I am used to say, "Do this," and it is done' (Ch. 13, p. 145).
- Jane is not intimidated or afraid of Rochester: 'I felt interested to see how he would go on' (Ch. 13, p. 142).
- Rochester is fascinated by Jane: 'I marvelled where you had got that sort of face' (Ch. 13, p. 143).
- Jane and Rochester appear to be on a similar wavelength straight away: '"The men in green all forsook England a hundred years ago," said I, speaking as seriously as he had done.' (Ch. 13, p. 144).

Task 2

- How much Jane admires Rochester: 'all energy, decision, will' (Ch. 17, p. 203).
- Blanche is shown to be arrogant and self-obsessed: 'She seems waiting to be sought' (Ch. 17, p. 204).
- Charlotte Brontë highlights the contrasts between Blanche and Jane with her descriptions of Blanche: 'she was evidently bent on striking them as something very dashing and daring indeed' (Ch. 17, p. 208).
- Jane feels completely alien and separate from the world she is observing: 'I then quitted my sheltered corner and made my exit by the side door, which was fortunately clear' (Ch. 17, p. 209).

PART THREE, page 63

SECTION ONE: CHECK YOUR KNOWLEDGE

1. John Reed
2. Mrs Fairfax
3. Bertha Rochester's brother/Rochester's brother-in-law
4. Grace Poole
5. Diana and Mary Rivers
6. Helen Burns
7. Adèle Varens
8. Miss Temple
9. Blanche Ingram
10. Bessie

SECTION TWO: CHECK YOUR UNDERSTANDING

Characters might include: Mrs Reed, Helen Burns, Miss Temple, Mrs Fairfax, Blanche Ingram, Diana and Mary Rivers, Rosamund Oliver, Bertha Rochester

What the relationship between Jane and this character is like: for example, Miss Temple is the first person to show Jane kindness and this has a very powerful effect on her: 'The kind whisper went to my heart like a dagger.' (Ch. 7, p. 78)

What Jane learns from this character: for example, Miss Temple shows the ability to challenge injustice: 'Miss Temple seemed to remonstrate' (Ch. 7, p. 76)

Jane recognises and admires the qualities Miss Temple possesses, which shows that she shares them: 'to her instruction I owed the best part of my acquirements' (Ch. 10, p. 100)

PART FOUR, PAGE 71

SECTION ONE: CHECK YOUR KNOWLEDGE

1. He believes that children are innately flawed and have to be 'corrected' in order to save their souls
2. She knows that Rochester does not love Blanche
3. She is concerned about the difference in their social status
4. She wants to marry for love rather than duty
5. It gets hit by lightning and broken in half
6. He wants to be a missionary
7. Being a governess
8. Because she is not willing to be his mistress
9. Jane
10. Because she is a devout Christian

The opening of the novel with the description of the weather: 'cold winter wind' and how this highlights Jane's loneliness and 'cold' treatment (Ch. 1, p. 9)

Jane's connection to the natural world and desire to be part of it: 'I wished the wind to howl more wildly' (Ch. 6, p. 65)

Charlotte Brontë's linking of the natural world with ideas of freedom: 'I am feverish: I hear the wind blowing: I will go out of doors and feel it' (Ch. 25, p. 317)

Brontë's use of symbolism: 'great horse-chestnut at the bottom of the orchard had been struck by lightning in the night, and half of it split away' (Ch. 23, p. 296)

PART FIVE, page 77

SECTION ONE: CHECK YOUR KNOWLEDGE

1. Jane Eyre
2. The lightning splitting the horse-chestnut tree in half
3. Five: Gateshead Hall, Lowood School, Thornfield Hall, Marsh End/Moor House, Ferndean Manor
4. The order in which events happen
5. Mr Rochester (fire), St John Rivers (ice)
6. Jane
7. A young child/baby
8. Past tense
9. First person
10. No, because she cannot see into the minds of the other characters

SECTION TWO: CHECK YOUR UNDERSTANDING

Jane as a young girl, lonely and isolated at Gateshead: 'I was a discord in Gateshead Hall' (Ch. 2, p. 19)

Jane learning about how to be peaceful and content from Miss Temple at Lowood: 'more harmonious thoughts; what seemed better regulated feelings had become the inmates of my mind' (Ch. 10, p.100)

Becoming a young adult but still has a lot to learn 'what is so headstrong as youth? What so blind as inexperience?' (Ch. 23, p. 281)

Learning to hold out for what she believes she can have, which is love and equality: 'I am my husband's life as fully as he is mine' (Ch. 38, p. 519)

MARK SCHEME

POINTS YOU COULD HAVE MADE

- Blanche's harsh descriptions of young men
- Her inability to show kindness or empathy
- Her concern with outward appearances
- Charlotte Brontë's use of irony – 'a pause which none interrupted' (Ch. 17, p. 208), etc.
- Use of language to show she sees marriage as some kind of battle: 'competitor' (Ch. 17, p. 208), etc.
- Her arrogant sense of self
- How Rochester clearly sees through Blanche
- The use of the fortune-teller to highlight Blanche's shallowness
- The contrast between Blanche and Jane

GENERAL SKILLS

Make a judgement about your level based on the points you made (above) and the skills you showed.

Level	Key elements	Spelling, punctuation and grammar	Tick your level
Very high	**A very well-structured answer which gives a rounded and convincing viewpoint.** You give a very detailed analysis of the writer's methods and the effects on the reader, using precise references which are fluently woven into what you say. You draw inferences, consider more than one perspective or angle, including the context where relevant, and make interpretations about the text as a whole.	You spell and punctuate with consistent accuracy, and use a very wide range of vocabulary and sentence structures to achieve effective control of meaning.	
Good to high	**A thoughtful, detailed response with well-chosen references.** At the top end, you address all aspects of the task in a clearly expressed way, and examine key aspects in detail. You are beginning to consider implications, explore alternative interpretations or ideas; at the top end, you do this fairly regularly and with some confidence.	You spell and punctuate with considerable accuracy, and use a considerable range of vocabulary and sentence structures to achieve general control of meaning.	
Mid	**A consistent response with clear understanding of the main ideas shown.** You use a range of references to support your ideas and your viewpoint is logical and easy to follow. There is some evidence of commenting on writers' effects though more is needed.	You spell and punctuate with reasonable accuracy, and use a reasonable range of vocabulary and sentence structures.	
Lower	**Some relevant ideas but an inconsistent and rather simple response in places.** You show you have understood the task and you make some points to support what you say, but the evidence is not always well chosen. Your analysis is a bit basic and you do not comment in much detail on the writer's methods.	Your spelling and punctuation is inconsistent and your vocabulary and sentence structures are both limited. Some of these make your meaning unclear.	